A Capital Upbringing

A Capital Upbringing

❖

Coming of Age in the 1930's in Montpelier, Vermont

Robert N. Webster

iUniverse, Inc.

New York Lincoln Shanghai

A Capital Upbringing
Coming of Age in the 1930's in Montpelier, Vermont

iUniverse, Inc.

For information address:
iUniverse, Inc.
2021 Pine Lake Road, Suite 100
Lincoln, NE 68512
www.iuniverse.com

Cover photo:
Bob Webster poses for a rare photograph in his first pair of long pants

ISBN: 0-595-33265-X

Printed in the United States of America

For Cameron, Lee, Kathy, Douglas, and Lynn

Contents

1

My earliest recollection was being punished for burying my mother's watch in a field behind our house. Mother was a telephone operator in the days when you placed all calls through one. You picked up the phone receiver that was separated from the phone by a cord and flicked the holder to get the operator's attention. She then asked whom you were calling or if you knew their number (usually of one or two digits). She then placed the call.

I have memories that are just brief flashes. I see in my mind's eye a time when I was in a crib and reached out to unscrew a light bulb in a lamp set on a table beside me. I then stuck a finger into the socket, and remember the sensation of shock. And in that same crib, I recall a blue bottle, which I assume was Vicks VapoRub. I also recall having someone beat flames off my pants in a yard somewhere. I recall a tiger kitten in the house on Ayers Street, but it is mixed with memories of Father pushing Mother around. I also remember seeing a sign on a neighbor's garage that said NOTICE and being perplexed because it was summer and there was no ice about. But these are just random thoughts and do not connect to anywhere or anyone or even any time.

Yet some true memories come back to me. The button incident occurred one day when I was quite young, I should say at the age of three or four. Mother had been sewing, and to keep me occupied while my new brother was sleeping in our bedroom, she showed me how to sew on a button by having me sew several onto a scrap piece of cloth. After many repeated attempts when I stuck myself with needles, I learned to sew the buttons on. Donald, my brother, awoke, and Mother rushed off to feed him, leaving me to my own devices. I had gotten really interested in my button sewing but, bored with using the same piece of cloth, I tried sewing one on an overstuffed chair. The material was quite stiff and pulled tight around the stuffing, so I had a hard time pulling the needle through. Then I spotted Mother's lace curtains and proceeded to sew a button on one side, which could be pulled through the loose lace pattern to button them together. By the time Mother returned, I had two sets buttoned together and was working on my third. This constituted my only experience with sewing until the service.

My father worked for the local gas company and managed the plant where the gas was made. Gas was made from coal or burning coke and was piped throughout the city to individual meters in each cellar. Twenty-five cents got you so many cubic feet of gas. When your gas stove or heater started to show yellow flame, down you went to the dark cellar and inserted your quarter for more gas.

My father worked days and my mother worked the late shift, so I was left for most of the day at my Grandmother Webster's house. Grandfather and Grandmother were from Aberdeen, Scotland, and still spoke Gaelic, and English with a thick brogue. They had come to the central Vermont area where there was a rather large enclave of Scottish immigrants, working mostly in the stone sheds of Barre, as that had been a major trade in Aberdeenshire.

Grandmother crocheted and had a group of Scottish ladies who met with her for tea every afternoon. They too crocheted and spent most of the afternoon conversing in Gaelic with Grandmother. The "Ladies" always referred to me as Bobie—not Bobbie—with the Scottish accent on "Bo", and made much of me at the teas. Gaelic became my first language up to the age of four. Mother finally took time off work to teach me English so I would be prepared for school, a real concern at that time, as we started school at age six. Happily not going to Grandmother's teas, and having Mother to myself for those two years, I did learn to speak and recognize English by the time school came.

I, of course, repaid her by becoming a pirate and burying her watch. In the way of all pirates, I promptly forgot where I stashed my loot and it was never found.

2

I remember my mother's mother singing the first few lines of the song *When Johnny Comes Marching Home Again*. I recall that she did this quite frequently and I had once asked her why.

It seems the tune had become popular in the United Kingdom and adopted as their own in England and Scotland in the late Victorian period while she was growing up in Aberdeen. It was played and sung often when troops left or returned during the Colonial Empire age. This and other songs she sang for me, frequently of a military nature, included clan tunes that told of tragic battles or lost loves of the highlands.

On a wall of our dining room was a small, hand-tinted, framed photograph. In it was a bridge built of broad stone with a high keystone arch under which a foam-flecked stream flowed. It was placed on an expanse of wall between two windows, the lone break in its plane. Sensing that it had some significance, I had asked as to its background story. Grandmother Ewen brightened immediately and told of the bridge's supposed magical properties when crossed as a couple, one boy, one girl. Passing under the arch was said to heighten romantic feelings and foretell an amorous future. Long life and good fortune was guaranteed them in the years ahead. There were claims for others who crossed this span as well. Kilted clansmen on their way to rival wars or raids on neighbor's cattle were assured of success.

The bridge was located somewhere to the west of Aberdeen in the Highlands: she described them as sloping, craggy mountains, with dense woods along the glens. She explained that she had visited the area and had seen the bridge itself. Whether she had walked its length alone or with someone she never noted and I guess I forgot to ask at the time. It was known as the brig of Belgounie. It became a source of mystery, putting wild and mysterious pictures in my child's mind.

Other times, she told macabre and morbid Scottish bedtime stories like *Wee Willie Winkle*, *The Worms Crawl In*, and *Black Douglas*, which sent shivers up my spine and left strange feelings about my Scottish heritage, not entirely diminished even today. Imagine a young child being regaled by such words as "the worms crawl in, the worms crawl out, they crawl all over your chin and snout", particularly just before the lights were turned off. It left me in terror of the darkness. I was also told that if I sinned in even the smallest way, Black Douglas would get me. Black Douglas was a cruel lord of ancient Scotland who tortured and murdered innocent subjects for the joy of it.

Wee Willie was a scoundrel whose passage threatened all sorts of crimes against the inhabitants, even bloody murder. I cannot remember the poem, but the feeling of intimidation still lingers.

My inquiries into ancestral relations were always answered in vagaries, with the exception of the MacWilliams side of our family. Our most prominent relation was one of the founders of the New College of Aberdeen University. Their coat of arms was emblazoned on the archway of the entrance to those ancient walls and his statue is in the courtyard of the Cathedral, she explained with Gaelic pride to my entranced ears. However, all questions about her life in the Old Country were passed over, as if their memory were too painful to relate even after so many years.

The only relationship she still held in some esteem was with some relative in Montreal by the name of Ogilvie whom she visited at intervals. Even then, she disclosed little about her trips except for the visits to the department store, a rather large establishment.

My memories of my maternal grandmother consist mostly of her matriarchal tendencies and playing cards with her friend Kate Colombo. If Kate came to our house to play, we were confined to the kitchen or back porch, allowed only quiet passage for toilet usage. We could just pick up the sounds of their play: the occasional laughter, bursts of frustrated low-key profanity, and the constant drumming of Kate's fingers on the dining room table. They were in tempo, incessant and loud, as if her thought process could not function without the marching, martial rhythm produced.

On those days when Grandmother Ewen was to visit and play at Kate's home, a deliberate pattern developed for the day. Having assigned the chores of the day to the various members of our household, she would retire to the second floor for a bath and meticulous ablutions before dressing in her finest. My memory of her figure receding up Foster Street to cross College on her way to Sabin Street where Kate resided is vivid even today. Hat perched correctly on her gray-haired head, shoes shining in the high-beamed sunlight, her pocketbook swaying from its strap set upon her shoulder, her gait still sprightly despite what I considered an ancient body, she strode purposefully into the distance until only the hat remained and then was gone from sight. I knew she would only return when the sun began to fade, in time for the supper she had planned that by now had been prepared by one of my aunts.

Perhaps the strongest influence she had on me were the habits I formed as a result of her stories. I only know that at an early age I could only sleep, and then with great apprehension, when I covered my head fully with blankets, leaving only the portion of my face required for breathing exposed to fresh air. It was not until my teens that I was able, by force of mind, to uncover my head and sleep as normal people do. Even in my advanced age, when the cold blasts of a frigid winter wind rattle the window panes or the flash of a summer storm's lightning repeatedly lights the room, that thoughts of Wee Willie or Black Douglas make me inch the covers higher and higher, until only my bald pate remains above them.

3

My Grandfather Webster was, as I vaguely recall, a rather large man, although his height was indeterminable; I looked up to everyone. He had a rather large waist (a Webster trait, apparently), and always wore a vest with a gold chain across it attached to a large pocket watch. I was particularly fascinated by the large elk tooth, which hung as a fob from the chain. He played a huge golden Irish harp that stood alongside his chair. On the other side was a crystal radio that stuttered and sizzled when playing, with its two dials on either side of a center window from where an amber light shone. Beside this sat a representation of the three virtues. Carved of soapstone were three monkeys, one with hands over its eyes, one with hands over its mouth, and one with hands over both ears—see no evil, hear no evil, and speak no evil. This I was not allowed to touch, although the elephant next to it, also made of soapstone, I was given to play with frequently.

Grandfather seemed to be retired or otherwise unemployed, as he was always in his chair when I arrived. Except for his timely approach to the bathroom, he sat Buddha-like eternally, listening to his radio to baseball games. Once in a while, when apparently there were no games being broadcast, he would arise, shrug on his jacket, reach for his straw hat, and announce that we (he and I) were going to take a walk. Grandmother would bring a sweater or jacket, depending on the temperature of the day, shrug me into it, making sure it was buttoned properly, and lead me to the door. Grasping my left hand in his, Grandfather and I would go down the stairs and out to the sidewalk to start our journey. With nods and hellos to neighbors we met, we would slowly climb the hill to Elmwood Cemetery which reposed at the top. Arriving at what to me was a vast plateau dotted with stones and statues of Barre granite, along which paths and roadways ran, Grandfather would pick a direction and we would proceed through that quiet place. Shrubs dotted the spaces beside the set stones, and occasionally a tree of some size sheltered the many birds that frequented the area, their songs and chirps sounding throughout the otherwise total quiet of the long plateau.

One incident stays clear in my mind to this day. Grandfather had stopped to show me a circling hawk that he had spotted just above the trees in front of us. Suddenly, the hawk swooped with folded wing. Grandfather let go of my hand and raced ahead to where the hawk had landed, leaving me behind. I, on short legs, ran to catch him, dodging around stones while he reached to the ground as the hawk rose away from him. As I gained ground to where he stood, I saw that he had retrieved something. When I approached him, he held out his cupped hands, in which lay a robin. The hawk had apparently attacked it on the ground. The robin's eyes were open, and it did not appear badly injured as Grandfather stroked it with a careful finger. Suddenly its wings flapped and it flew from his hands, upward to a branch in a large tree not far away. Grandfather laughed as I stood in amazement, and said in a serious tone, "He didn't get you after all. You seem to be all right." Grandfather had arrived before the hawk could seriously injure the bird, and in my child's mind was accorded hero status for his act.

Unfortunately, we had few moments together after the robin incident; he died that winter of a heart attack. The last impression I have is of him reposed in the casket before which I was held to say good-bye. He had died "of fat around the heart."

4

My paternal grandmother was quite different from my maternal one, being of a more jovial nature. She was short and rotund in the Webster mode, with a gregarious nature shown to all she knew. She exuded motherly traits, which she bestowed freely to all under her care.

Not to say she was perfect. Indeed, the Celtic curse afflicted her as well as my grandfather and their offspring. In fact, the whisky bottle appeared on her table with the very first meal of the day, there to repose until she and Grandfather had partaken of its contents by day's end. Only on those days when her Scottish friends gathered to speak their native Gaelic tongue and tat the afternoons away was the bottle whisked to a cupboard until company departed. Then it was brought forth to make up for lost time as they ate supper.

She was, at least to me, attentive and loving. I stayed with her those days my mother worked and was the only one I remember who hugged me to her ample body whenever I entered her realm. It seems in my waning memory of those years that until school changed the pattern of my days, the ladies who came to tat called me Bobie in a thick Scots brogue. I would answer in Gaelic (long since forgotten) as they leaned into their work of needles and threads, whether tatting or crocheting in rhythm about the room.

On one wall hung a framed and glassed Gold Star on a white field with red borders. The Gold Star signified the loss of a son during World War I. My Gramie showed great pride and animation when I asked her about it. In fact, if no mention were made on my part, she would bring it up, and elaborate in detail. Her eldest son Bert's death on the Western Front brought her sorrow but also became, I think, the essence of Gramie's life from that time on. In my early years, of course, none of what she said meant anything to me, but as I came into my teens, my mind began to comprehend their meaning.

It seems as though every time I visited her I was given the whole story about my Uncle Bert; all the gory details about his demise were repeated with pride above the ordinary. Being a Gold Star Mother, she, along with hundreds of others, were shipped to France some time after the end of the Great War to visit the graves of their lost offspring at full government expense. She showed me pictures of her trip: the liner she shipped on, the cemetery archway with those stark-white crosses. One showed a smiling Gramie standing to the right of Bert's memorial cross, dressed in black from hat to suit to shoes. In time I realized that in all her life this was the very topmost thing she had ever experienced or would from that trip on. It was, perhaps, the only thing that had given her attention and pride in an otherwise mundane existence. All I have of Bert is a certificate stating that Robert Webster, my namesake, died serving his nation.

She lost my grandfather in the 1930's, and for the rest of her life she lived with Uncle Cecil. Uncle James went to California, and eventually my father and mother were divorced, with Lester heading to Canada.

To me, she was always Gramie with her hugs on my visits by bus from Montpelier, until my final visit just before going into the service. She passed away while I served my time. One of my first acts on arriving back home was to visit her grave where she rests in Hope Cemetery.

Today, having lived to an age I never expected to reach, I look back on that humble, loving soul, remembering all her kindness to me. I thank whatever Gods there be for having known her in my youth. I still see the photo in my mind's eye of a smiling, though mourning grandmother, and I still associate her with those crosses, row on row.

5

My father was a small man in stature, having a height of about 5'8"—the smallest of the clan. Cecil, my uncle, was perhaps an inch taller, but made up for height with breadth. To look at him, you would calculate him to be as broad as he was tall. Jim, the oldest, was also the tallest at six feet, with a serious nature and not much personality.

All of the Webster side of the family drank hard and daily. Even Grandmother and Grandfather began the day with a bottle on the table, starting as soon as breakfast was finished. Only in later years did Grandmother, Cecil, and James quit. All of their friends were the same, taking Celtic pride in how much their bodies could take, both of liquor and pain from their fraternal fights. Perhaps it was the times—depression times in more ways than one. Father had a problem with alcohol that he never conquered. He was friendly and easygoing when sober, but became an irascible, nasty drunk when in his cups.

There were good times, like Sunday picnics after a long drive. I remember him taking me to ballgames occasionally and to the local swimming hole, which was behind a dam on the Steven's Branch of the Winooski River with sand on one edge for a type of beach, and a very shallow area for young children. We were well supervised by high school-age female lifeguards, so we could play in the shallow water with abandon.

Once Father took me to a camp on Woodbury Pond with some friends of his. Of course, the liquor flowed freely in the camp. Father gathered me up, walked to the end of their dock and threw me in, which was evidently his way of teaching me to swim. I was supposed to instinctively know to thrash my arms. Naturally, I sunk like a heavy rock to the bottom. Lucky for me a friend in slightly more sober attitude noticed and dove in to rescue me. That brought to a close my swimming lesson, and it was never attempted again. It also brought about a change in my father, as he avoided water for the rest of his life, sticking mainly to an alcohol diet.

One day, Father, Uncle Cecil and I were stuffed into Father's Model-A Ford work truck for a trip to some unremembered destination. Model-A's were notoriously small, and had but one seat each for the driver and passenger. Father and Cecil had been imbibing quite liberally all morning and were in no shape to drive. However, there we were, driving up toward Plainfield from Barre on a winter's day. Due to Cecil's size, I was relegated to his lap, as there was no room even to fit little me in beside them. In those days, seat belts were unheard of, so in the event of an accident, all one could do was hang on to whatever one could.

As we accelerated to make the slight grade, the wheels spun on ice formed under a new snowfall. We turned a circle and a half and crashed dead center into a tree on the border of the other roadside. I, of course, accelerated into the windshield as Cecil tried to hold both him and me to the seat. Blood spurted from my nose and a gash on my head and I howled at the top of my lungs. In due course, Father and Cecil got out of the truck, Cecil still holding me. Father and he yelled at each other and then Father struck Cecil, claiming he had not protected me enough. Cecil, in turn, referred to Father's driving as terrible and claimed that he was to blame. Cecil gave me a cursory exam and set me down in the roadway as the two of them continued their argument.

The truck, meanwhile, was slowly turning against the tree and sliding toward the steep bank beyond. A man came along and pointed this out to the still-arguing pair. They rushed to the truck and stopped its slide. With the help of the man, they managed to push the truck back to the roadway facing back the way we came. The man pulled out his handkerchief and dabbed the blood from my cut and my bleeding nose, admonished my father and uncle, and went on his way. Back in the truck, which didn't have any apparent damage other than the radiator whose fumes permeated the air with alcohol antifreeze, we went back down the grade, eventually returning home. Mother took one look at me, was properly put out, and told my father and uncle so.

Looking back over the years, it seems to me we were fortunate indeed to have survived that accident. We could easily have missed the tree and gone over the embankment, which at that point was perhaps thirty feet high. I, as I recall, was not hurt badly and recovered that afternoon. It stayed with me that alcohol and ice make a bad combination, not to mention the horrid smell released from a cracked radiator.

With my father's drinking problem came fights with his brothers and my mother. I remember being at Grandmother's house, playing with a new toy car on Grandmother's bed, when one of the spats between my father and Uncle Cecil spilled into the bedroom. Both were well oiled at the time and intent on doing bodily harm. My father pushed Cecil and all 300-plus pounds landed on my hand, with the new metal car under it. Naturally, it cut my hand, and his weight compounded the problem. Grandmother managed to extricate me and carry me to the kitchen where she ministered to both my hand and my feelings as best she could while berating both participants, who by now had come out of their fog of alcoholic rage.

Mother had long put up with Father coming home in a belligerent state, and even the birth of my younger brother did little to alleviate the situation. Finally, one Sunday she packed up, having had enough, as my father slept in his chair in the living room in a stupor, and we left in a taxi to go to Montpelier and my other grandparents' home. So we left Barre behind with its sad memories and acquaintances: the Bellas (Auntie Bella, my grandmother's sister and Aunt Bella, Cecil's wife), my cousins, the Cummings—Francis, Bobby, and David—and the numerous tough schoolmates I had feared in my extreme youth.

My first and second year teacher at Ayers Street School in Barre had also taught my father in his youth. She might have been a good teacher—which I can't remember. All I know is that she terrified us all with her long-handled spoon, a large kitchen-type about fourteen inches long, and her penchant for locking us in a closet for discipline for long periods in complete isolation with no light to warm the walls. The spoon, by the way, was applied with vigor to out-stretched palms of students who were forced to stand in front of her. How she managed not to break bones is a mystery. She certainly seemed to enjoy the act.

My fellow students ran in gangs and, since I belonged to none, I was prime meat every day. I took many beatings in the time I spent at that school and was happy to leave it behind. There were a few good memories, such as picnics on Sundays and parades of old vets on July 4th, swimming in the Winooski River, and times with my cousins, but somehow they pale in the misery of my family's drinking and the ultimate fatherless divorce. My maternal grandparents were also of Celtic stock, but decidedly more Calvinistic in thought. Alcohol was not a problem in their everyday life, except for one uncle who was a devoted disciple of the grape.

6

So my mother, brother Donald, and I joined a group already enlarged by divorce. My two cousins, William and Barbara, had both joined this clan prior to us, setting the precedent. The characters of this "family" came to include: Grandmother Ewen, Grandfather Ewen; Aunts Edith, Nonie, Katherine, and Roberta (Buddy), my mother's sisters; cousins William and Barbara; my mother Jessie, Donald, and myself; and a sometimes supplemental foster child, Nancy.

All were domiciled within one side of a huge house on a dirt street in Montpelier. This consisted of a large kitchen, dining room and living room on the first floor, adjacent to a foyer of sorts, which took up about the same area as half the living room. A porch the size of the kitchen located right next to it hung suspended a good fifteen feet above the ground. Steel pillars held it up, and part of the under section was finished as a wood room. Passing up the stairs to the second floor, which served as a roof for the cellar stairs, a long hallway stretched from the stair top to the front bedrooms. Straight ahead from the stairs was a door to bedroom #1; next to that in the hallway was a bathroom, and beyond was another bedroom, until you reached the front bedroom with a den adjacent to it. Across the hall from the second bedroom, a door opened onto massive stairs that led to a landing, then turned as a normal staircase to the attic, which consisted of three small bedrooms off a small hall. My brother and I were integrated with our cousins in bedroom #1, while Mother was placed in an attic room. Donald and I followed to the bedroom next to hers as soon as beds could be purchased for us.

Our house must have been built in the late 1800's, taking into consideration both its size and general architecture. It was painted a cream yellow with a lead based white trim paint—one coat of paint on the front and sides. The back was left unpainted, as were most houses built in that era. Heavily checked paint clung perilously to weathered boards impregnated by granite dust, ravaged by sun and weather.

Huge granite blocks stacked to a height of over eight feet enclosed a dirt-floored cellar and held the hewn sills in place. Since the land dropped off at the juncture of the dining room and kitchen, a walled back extended a floored room used as a food cellar that ran under the kitchen. This usually was filled with jars of canned goods in the form of tomatoes, carrots, peas, beans and more beans, which glittered in the soft light of a 40 watt bulb suspended by a long cord from the ceiling. Also aligned on the shelves were bottles of root beer, survivors of the last year's bottling. On hot, humid days, the afternoon sun would penetrate through the single window in the back wall and heat the bottles. Explosions could occasionally be heard upstairs in the kitchen as the bottles broke, sounding like a rifle range below. Kids would try surreptitiously to slip away before someone sent them down to clean up the resulting mess. Being the largest of the children, I was usually spontaneously elected janitor of the cellar, as the adults tended to spot me first. I soon learned to absent myself from the house on hot humid days.

The McNeils, another Celtic family, occupied the other side of the house, which was the mirror image of our side. The rest of the neighborhood consisted of Italian, Greek, and Slavic families, and one Swedish and one French for good measure.

Only three people in our entire area of the city had an automobile. Guido Magne and Frank Facini had second hand Model-A Fords and George Seivwright had a new Chrysler, one in a line of many in the years to come. The streets were either made of packed gravel or, with our proximity to the stone sheds, granite dust. Granite dust made a fine looking road, being white in color when applied liberally over a gravel bed. However, it did have its drawbacks, as all unpaved roads do. It made an excellent surface when wet, but when dry for several days in hot sunshine it lay in wait for a good breeze or traffic to release clouds of dust that covered everything within striking distance. Many words best not heard by children colored the air along with the dust as neighbors hung out their laundry to be coated gray-white with the fine surface of our streets. Fortunately, most of our street mates used their tongue of origin when venting their anger and it was several years before their children had diligently taught us the finer parts of their languages.

We were situated on the south side of what was known at the time as Seminary Hill. It got its name from the group of buildings dotted around an open space, or square, which housed Montpelier Seminary, a secondary school operated by the Methodist Church. Most of the wooden buildings incorporated in the school were old Civil War barracks, left from a hospital used during that war. A large brick structure of imposing late-19th century architecture, complete with a large bell tower rising from its center archway, had been added. Directly in front of the main entrance, on a slight rise from the flat field that formed a large square, was a fountain made of granite that contained a round pool, with an ornate tiered cast iron spire that spewed water in graceful curves to fall in the water below. Huge elms, interspersed with large maple trees, lined the square and the pathways on either side of the central building.

Homes surrounded the square and dotted a rather precipitous hill that led all the way to the Winooski River several hundred feet below. The side of this great mound was cleaved with three roads that led straight down to the riverside. Crossing these was one road, Foster Street, about halfway down the incline. This was where our house sat clinging to a partial terrace formed by the street. Trolley tracks centered the roads leading from the middle of the capital city, up East State Street to the campus, connecting with tracks on College Street, and continuing past the dormitory barracks lining the east side of the plateau to turn down a curve that led around the hill and gradually swung to meet the abrupt end of College Street again, then down to Barre Street along the riverside.

Poles bearing telephone and electric lines stood like double barrel crucifixes in line with all the streets. Bulbed lamps with circular shields shone at night from strategically placed spots here and there on these splintery posts. We were either fortunate or unfortunate, depending on your viewpoint, to have one directly in front of our house. At night, it shone in our windows with either a disturbing glare or friendly glow, depending where your bedroom window was located. Of course, it helped to delay our bedtime by artificially lighting the area so we could continue outdoor games, such as Kick the Can or Stick.

Kick the Can or Kick the Stick were played by choosing one unfortunate child to guard the can or stick leaning against the pole, while the rest hid behind trees or porches, within agreed limits of the area. The guard could roam somewhat, as his job was to find and tag the hidden kids coming to kick the stick or can. If the guard tagged a child before reaching the goal, he or she became the guard in turn, relieving the former guard and allowing him or her to join the hiding children. Of course, if the child coming to the goal could avoid the tag and kick the can or stick, the guard retained his or her post.

This became very argumentative and judges had to be appointed on the spur of the moment to decide whether the kick was first or the tag. Long discourses ensued until resolved either by the judges or the local mothers calling us in to prepare for bed. If a guard tired of the game or the mothers called, the guard would yell "Ollie-Ollie in Free!" and the game would be over. We played other games, of course. Having a high bank opposite the house, King of the Hill was popular with all the neighborhood kids.

Mother, Donald, and I had settled in quite well and, as I gathered from grown-up talk, Mother had filed for divorce. My father was nowhere to be found. We discovered much later that he had left the state and gone to Canada, where he stayed with relatives unknown to me even now. Later, he joined the Canadian Army, and served throughout World War II. He joined the Victoria Rifles in Western Canada, where he again stayed with relatives. I always thought that his fleeing to Canada may in part have been motivated by a dislike of alimony and child support; however, I expect that instead he took the slogan "Drink Canada Dry" to heart. It always bothered me that he did not think enough of my brother and me to stay and face up to his responsibilities.

So I soon drifted into a typical Depression childhood like millions of others and grew up in an age where not having material things hardly mattered.

7

Grandfather Ewen was a tall slim man made almost skeletal by the ravages of silicosis, a disease similar to tuberculosis caused by granite dust in vast quantities, a common condition among stone cutters who worked in the granite sheds at that time. The pneumatic drills used to cut the stone into its rough monument shapes sprayed clouds of the dust into the air. Men wore kerchiefs over their noses and mouths that were very ineffective at keeping the dust from their lungs. Goggles of a sort protected the eyes, but the kerchiefs only partially blocked the nasal passages and mouths of the cutters. Large quantities of dust were inhaled into the lungs, irritating the lung tissue and creating pockets, which became inflamed and infected with bacteria. Grandfather lay in the front bedroom day and night listening to the radio or puffing his helpful Old Gold cigarettes. It was only a short time until he, too, lay in an open casket in the living room, and I had lost my second grandfather before I really got to know him.

The living room had sliding doors that pulled out from the partitions to meet in the center of an archway. They were closed most of the time, as we children were not allowed there except on special occasions, such as the viewing of a relative who had passed on, Christmas, and days when special company came, when we were admonished not to touch anything. It was impossible to do this to the letter as we walked on the rug, sat in chairs (if any were available), and occasionally picked things up to examine them. Many times I was asked harshly to leave the room, and it got so that I would just pull a dining room chair to the edge of the archway, there to sit and observe—but not, God forbid, to touch!

The Calvinist attitude of this side of my family caused all children to be relegated to the kitchen at some time, occasionally to be joined by one of my aunts when my iron-willed grandmother did not approve her behavior. I don't mean to say that I disliked her. On the contrary, I loved her as all grandchildren love their grandparents. It was only that she had created a matriarchal system for this family, in part, I assume, because of my grandfather's long illness, and the necessity of having to take over as head of the household. For whatever reason, Grandmother ruled the roost. Whenever she was or thought she was defied, she turned to her enforcer, my Aunt Edith. Edith was a large woman, solid on her feet, and efficient as Grandmother's disciplinarian. Her physical prowess cowed all before her.

Grandmother either knitted or crocheted, usually afghans, went off to shop, or to Kate Colombo's to play cards of an afternoon, a routine never broken except on holidays or when the weather was inclement. Edith did housework in a few of the more affluent homes in the city. She was also Grandmother's official cook, especially on Sundays. Her meals were sensational even by today's standards. It was not uncommon to have Sunday guests for dinner, and it was considered a privilege to be invited to partake of the feast. This was made possible by the largess of Ma Bell, in the form of salaries, as all the women in the family worked for the telephone company. They paid regularly into the household account administered by Grandmother.

In Montpelier, you either worked for the granite manufacturers, the National Life Insurance Company, the State of Vermont, or the telephone company. The elite were high management of the National Life and, of course, upper levels of the state government. The underlings in both these organizations were compensated for their labors with a much smaller amount of both pay and prestige. Linemen for the telephone company made what was considered above average salaries, and operators were at the bottom of the company scale. Granite workers made what was considered adequate pay for their labors. Since the country was deep into the Great Depression, with the NRA (National Recovery Act) and CCC (Civilian Conservation Corps) in effect to employ the hoards of people out of work, anyone lucky enough to be employed did not want to lose their situation.

Labor was looked upon as being Communist and abhorred by management. Consequently, labor was at a low point at this particular time. The CCC was organized like the military, even to the point of wearing surplus World War I clothing. They built flood control dams, recreation fields and parks, municipal swimming pools and roads, and were a vivid part of our lives for many years. The NRA, besides enabling the CCC, paid for all its projects and others, which was necessary in order to fill the needs of our battered country.

Once we were warned not to go down to Barre Street where the laborers were on strike in the granite sheds. We kids in the neighborhood knew nothing about strikes, so when the fire alarm sounded, we sneaked down to where we could see the sheds from the side hill. There were gangs of men in work clothes gathered on Granite Street, shouting and carrying clubs made of two-by-fours or pipe in their hands. That scared us enough to send us running home so that we didn't see what happened. We heard years later that this strike ended peacefully. Some, however, were not peaceful and ended in property damage and personal injury. George Seivwright, my friend Jim's father, lost an eye in one of them. The National Guard was called out on many of them. Eventually, through the years, conditions improved. Pay hikes were given, silicosis was generally defeated, and the sanatorium in Barre was closed. Walkouts continued for many years, however, and although they were not violent, they still caused tough times for the workers.

My Aunt Nonie was a dark beauty and was not often around, due to being squired by a bevy of suitors. She was, however, very cordial when she was with the children. Aunt Katherine was the most jovial of the group and was often the butt of our pranks. In particular, she had an almost hysterical fear of insects, spiders, June bugs and the like. Gathered of a summer's evening on our vine-covered front porch, someone would inevitably find one of these and sneak behind her to try to drop it down her back. This brought shrieks and windmilling arms as she stood and shook to dislodge the offending bug. Although she soon composed herself and berated us thoroughly for the offense, she soon laughed along with us. How she put up with us, I'll never understand. Yet, as we all got older, we respected her for her good humor and loved her more because of her tolerance.

Aunt Roberta, known as Buddy, was the youngest of the girls still in school and closer in age to us. She became a mentor to me, and I spent a lot of time talking to her about all subjects. I would say I was closer to her than the others simply because she took the time to talk to me and listened to me when I had problems or needed answers.

My Uncle William, whom we rarely saw since he did not live with us, was an enigma to me. I think he worked as a plumber, along with his friend Chuck McDermott, although I was never sure of this. My recollection of him was mostly his playing baseball for the semi-pro club who played their home games at the National Life field. They owned a large plot of land bordered by what was then Winooski Avenue on one side and by the Winooski River on the other. Uncle Bill was a very good ball player, and was quite well known and respected for it in the community.

My only sharp memory of him was unfortunate. I had sassed one of my aunts at a time when he was at the house, and had gotten my face slapped by him, along with a short lecture on keeping my thoughts to myself when spoken to by an adult. I learned a lesson that day, but was also left with a bitter memory that haunts me to this one. Bill was killed early in World War II.

8

Starting school in the Montpelier system was an experience for me, in some ways good and some ways bad. Most of my fellow classmates had started school together in kindergarten and I was a stranger among them. On the other hand, we were all starting in another building since they went only through grade two in the primary school, then moved to the Washington County Grammar School for grade three, which put us all in the same situation. The teachers were of a better nature than I was used to, and all discipline problems were referred to the Principal.

It didn't take too long to be integrated into the class and to make new friends. My first day was uneventful as we went through a sort of orientation where we were shown the school and assigned seats and cloakroom hangers on which to hang our coats or jackets. The second day was more what I was used to: the bullyboys asserted themselves and I had three short fights where I gained an instant reputation as tough. The bullies decided it was too hard on them and left me alone after that.

School itself holds few memories for me at that stage in my life. Only the summer vacations linger in my mind. Trips to Sabin's pasture to catch frogs and minnows and the occasional garter snake, baseball and football on the back campus of the Seminary, and playing in the neighborhood are vivid recollections that have stayed with me. Meanwhile, life was just a series of school and vacations, with an occasional event thrown in to pique our interests. In 1937, the King and Queen of England visited Canada and the United States. In school we were told of this monumental occasion and our teachers made much of the trip.

Our lives revolved more immediately around events in the neighborhood. The neighborhood had several ethnic groups within its boundaries and we learned a lot from each other. The fathers, when not working, all fished and hunted in season and gardened to supplement their meager salaries. Everyone had a garden in back of his or her house. Many built up land contained by walls of scrap granite. Since the land on our hillside consisted of heavy clay, bluish in color and hard as rock, our gardens were filled with loads of loam obtained from farmers in the Montpelier and East Montpelier areas. Walls, some six to eight feet in height, were made on hillsides, and then leveled with the dirt brought in by wagonload.

Everyone had an old barrel, usually of wood, in which a mix of cow manure and water was kept. Particularly in the spring, the smell of manure permeated the neighborhood as the men mixed the loam and fertilizer by shovel to prepare for planting.

Special pride was taken in growing tomato plants, the size of the tomatoes and the number on each plant of great importance. They were protected, fertilized, and watered with loving care, suckers picked, and plants staked with sticks and cloth ties, covered with cheesecloth and watched with jealous eyes by others. Rivalries were established that flamed bright, particularly at harvest time. Of course, other vegetables were grown and they also fueled this friendly rivalry. Zucchini, in particular, were measured by size, the larger the better. Peas, beans, carrots, cauliflower, beets, beans and more beans were all "canned" in glass jars with rubber seals and glass covers. Canning season was a hot steamy time in all kitchens. Tomatoes were eaten off the vine or the surplus canned. Some tomatoes were dried on screens for use in sauces in the winter. Herbs, parsley in particular, were dried in bundles tied together and hung from the porch ceiling to sway in the breeze.

The full moon, which rose either in late August or early September, was the signal for wild mushroom harvest. Children soon learned to distinguish good from bad mushrooms. In Vermont, the most common good mushroom was the Belita. Its large cap, solid base and sponge-like bottom identified this fungus from others. Found in areas of spruce trees with moss-covered ground, the same area in which snowshoe hares abounded, the hunt was anticipated with great excitement. The children dragged bushel peach baskets to where two or three mushrooms were found under tree branches. Sometimes seven or eight in a clump would be spied, and the law of first come, first served prevailed. You did not pick someone else's find, and they in turn respected yours. Many days were spent in the sport and bushel upon bushel were brought home. Then the work would begin.

All the mushrooms were washed in cold water, then set on tables, usually on the porches, where they were prepared for canning or drying. The stems were broken from the caps and peeled or scraped. Then with a small sharp blade they were cut into strips the long way. The caps had to be scooped of their spongy bottoms, then cut in strips as well. They were then rewashed in lightly salted water. Drying the mushrooms was a problem because they had to be in a dry, well-aired place. The inside corner of the porch was used and the racks of screens built up with spaces between to let air through. If you were lucky, you had clear warm weather, and after a few days of turning the mushrooms would be thoroughly dry. They were then placed in jars or tins for storage in the cellar room alongside all the canned goods.

Fishing and hunting were also an important supplement to everyone's diets. Of particular interest were the snowshoe hare and the ruffed grouse, or partridge, as it is known in Vermont. Every able-bodied man hunted in season (and sometimes out of season). Several men in the neighborhood kept beagles or larger crossbred hounds that were trained on rabbits. Since they were used only for hunting, they were kept chained to a doghouse or enclosed in a fenced area with a shelter inside. They were never left to run loose, as this supposedly diminished their hunting instincts. Keeping them restrained somehow was supposed to make them more eager to hunt when they were finally unleashed in the woods. They stayed outdoors in all weather. Even when the thermometer dropped to 20 or 30 below or the heat of high summer peaked, they suffered within their confines. I must admit they were always eager and ran all day when allowed to hunt.

The dogs would usually work the edges of a swampy area surrounded by spruce or balsam fir woods. Once they had scented a rabbit, off they would go baying on the trail. Snowshoe rabbits have a propensity to circle an area about a half mile in diameter, and the role of the hunter is to find the approximate path of the chased prey, find an open spot, and wait listening to the dogs baying toward the hunter. Alert to motion ahead of the dogs, the hunter spies the rabbit and shoots the racing hare with a shotgun. Occasionally, a buck hare would circle once or twice and then head for the mountaintops to circle once or twice there before returning to the woods.

Fall hunting was a pleasant affair. Usually the weather was typical autumn—cold mornings; warm, clear, blue-skied middays; and cool again toward evening. Winter was another story with either lowering skies and snow, or clear, crisp, cold short days. We hunted in all kinds of weather. Being cold and wet was a common thing as our clothing of the day was not as warm as the new fibers of today.

We wore long underwear, wool pants and shirts and wool socks. Our feet were enclosed in leather boots we called high-cuts that fit tightly as they laced up all the way to their tops, stopping just below the knees. Johnson pants made at the Johnson Woolen Mill, made like old-time cavalry pants, laced from the bottom of the shin to the knee, and then ballooned out to the waist. Wool and leather are fine at 30 or 40 degrees, but when wet, both allow water to pass through. Pushing through snow, even on a day with temperatures in the 30's, with both wet boots and pants, you noticed when the sun slid behind the mountains, the cold penetrating deep into your bones.

Fishing was much more pleasant as the weather kept us warm, except in early spring. Most of my fishing was in a brook or river, with an occasional trip to a lake or pond. My day started by waking at four or five o'clock in the morning, sneaking downstairs so I wouldn't wake anyone else. After a quick breakfast of cereal and milk, I would make a sandwich, usually peanut butter and jelly. Gathering my telescoping pole and other tackle, I would head out. Walking the railroad tracks to East Montpelier Village, I would fish back to Montpelier, usually at the foot of the dams and their races. Rainbow and brown trout abounded in the Winooski in those days. Usually by two o'clock I would have two or three nice fish and be heading back down the tracks to home.

On some days, I would head for Paradise Brook, so named for the dance hall built beside where it crossed the Barre Road. Up Berlin Street, I would go in total darkness to the Berlin Town line where the brook crossed under the road and I would fish down to the Barre Road. It was a small stream, but deep in places where it flowed in the divide of pastureland and woods at the bottom. It held brook trout in its deeper pools and yielded many a good catch to me.

Another brook I fished was called Benjamin Falls Brook. It started at a dam that held the Montpelier Reservoir and ended in the Steven's Branch after flowing under the Barre Road by the State Garage. Sometimes I would climb what we called Clay Hill to the Riding Club Brook that flowed from the Morse Farm on the County Road, crossed Murray Road and again crossed Towne Hill Road to flow into the Winooski by Plant #3. These also yielded good catches of brook trout. The Winooski River at the confluence of the North Branch in Montpelier had large perch and bull pout which we caught by fishing from shore. The Dog River from Riverton down to the Winooski had rainbow and brown trout, which I fished occasionally. We thought nothing in those days of walking three, four, even seven miles out to find a good fishing spot, usually measuring distances by dams. Everyone knew where we could be found on a good fishing day.

At this time in my life, I had become friends with one of my neighbors of my own age, Dick Comolli. His family lived in a house on Sibley Avenue that backed our house. The Comolli's were nice people and, although I saw little of Dick's father, his mother was a great person. Dick and I liked the same things and got along great. Dick got a bicycle for Christmas one year and from then on until we were too big for it the two of us used it to transport us to fishing places. I rode the handlebars and Dick pedaled us everywhere, as he was the larger.

One day, we had played out the fish in Paradise Brook. Because he had ridden the bike up the hill in the morning, we could coast all the way down to River Street. As we went down the hill, Dick applied the brakes often to keep our speed down. Because of the weight of both of us on the bike, it became increasingly difficult to slow us down. As we approached the Marvin Creamery, something snapped loudly. The chain had broken during our braking and had it not been for Dick's quick thinking, we would have shot out onto River Street into traffic. Dick bailed us into the garden beyond the creamery, where we cleaned out beanpoles and tomato stakes until we finally slowed and toppled off. What saved us was the fact that the garden had recently been rototilled by the owner, softening the ground. Neither of us was injured except for bumps and bruises, which we always had anyway, but the garden was totaled. We spent many days repairing the damage for the irate owner. The house with the garden was later to belong to my Aunt Katherine and her second husband Unc.

9

A wood furnace heated our house with a central grate in the dining room, and perimeter registers in all rooms except the attic where Donald, Mother and I slept. On exceedingly cold nights, we were allowed to leave the attic door ajar so as to allow a little heat into our attic bedrooms. Most of the time, water left in a glass at the bedside would freeze by morning. We piled on the blankets and slept with only our chins and noses exposed to the elements.

Wood cut in four-foot lengths would be dumped in a pile beside the house. It was my job, as I grew older to cut these into pieces to accommodate the furnace. I would set up the sawhorse, struggle to lay up the log, and then proceed to cut it with a bucksaw. Night after night, in all kinds of weather, I would cut the cord wood until it was all cut up, thrown in the cellar, and stacked along the outside walls, all the time envying my brother and cousins who were not big enough for the job. Sometimes Buddy, more often Katherine, would help with the stacking in the cellar, but mostly it was left to me alone.

Edith was keeper of the fire and it was she who loaded the furnace and kept the ashes in a large washtub for me to dispose of, usually in the garden to help sweeten the soil. Most of the time we made it through the winter with this supply. However, there were times when in March a smaller load was brought to get us through spring, and it was very unpleasant due to the extreme cold to be cutting at night. I had to rush home after school and do the job before supper. I really hated this period and never seemed to be warm except when bundled in bed. My feet in my highcuts and hands in soggy wet woolen mittens would be white from the cold when I finally had to quit for supper. Then I would bring a chair to the stove, open the oven and stick my feet in until they had thawed before I ate. I shivered until bedtime.

Once when I was about ten or eleven years old, I had joined the Scouts and had a meeting after school at the Curtis house. I came home late, at about seven o'clock. This displeased my Grandmother Ewen and she had Edith lock me out. When I knocked on the kitchen door to be let in, I was informed by "The Enforcer" that I was to stay out. It was below zero, a night so cold and crisp that snow squeaked and crackled underfoot, and I didn't know what to do. My mother was in the house, as well as all the rest of the family, and made no attempt to get me in away from the cold. I have never forgiven any of them for their cowardly position taken that night.

I had my winter clothes on, including my highcuts, which by then encased two clubs of frozen feet. When I stood still, the cold permeated my whole body and I shivered uncontrollably. Only by moving about could I stop the shivering. I finally wandered off up over the hill to the college, walking around the campus because I kept warmer doing so. Sometime after ten p.m., as I was walking by the old tennis courts, Jerry, Jim Seivwright's dog, caught up to me. As I was petting him, George Seivwright, Jim's father, came up to us and in total shock asked what I was doing there at that hour. I told him what had happened and he took me to his house to bed for the night. Evidently he also called my grandmother and read her the riot act and the next morning he accompanied me home where he re-lectured all concerned. That was the end of the incident. George Seivwright very probably saved my life.

Winter seemed colder in those days, probably because we did not have the protective clothing that we have today. We still played every day after school in the immense snow banks that lined the streets and covered what sidewalks we had. Snow removal was unheard of at that time and snow was just piled up high by the plows that were powered by teams of horses. We made tunnels with carved-out rooms and held candles for light to see by. All streets in those days were plowed, but not salted or even sanded, so we could slide anywhere, except for some dangerous ones that were posted with No Sliding signs. We used all manner of sliding apparatus—flyer sleds, jumpers, traverses, and toboggans.

Jumpers were made of barrel staves nailed to an upright with a cross piece nailed on top for a seat. We had to exercise caution and learn to balance in order to ride one. Traverses were large affairs with a high flat base supported by a set of back runners and steered by a jointed set of runners that swiveled so you could steer with your feet as you sat upon it. It had room for four or five people, who were needed to pull it up hills, as it was quite heavy. The runners were of shaped steel and kept polished for speed. The wood was either white ash or oak, depending on which part of the county you obtained it. Ours was of ash and must have weighed eighty to one hundred pounds. All these were made to slide on packed snow, so the streets were perfect. The toboggan and jumper worked as well in the fields and hills, even in non-packed snow.

Bingham Street was a road that dropped sharply from East State Street to cross Marvin, and then curved upward to Liberty Street. It was later posted, I am sure, because of what happened to me. There were about five of us, and someone had dared the rest to go down Bingham on sleds. Naturally, we all took off one after another, rocketing down to the intersection of the streets.

My cousin Billy was in front of me by about twenty feet as he crossed the Marvin Street intersection, and it was then that I saw something out of the corner of my eye. Suddenly, the hood of a large truck loomed in front of me and the next thing I knew I was under the truck body. I was going so fast that before the back wheels got to me, I shot out the other side and up to Liberty where I stopped by steering into a large snow bank. We never repeated the slide again. I am sure that, for once, I had extraordinary luck or the will of God on my side for, thinking back, if I had been a split second slower, or if the truck had been going faster, I would not be telling this.

Later in our teens we took to skiing and ski jumping. Our skis were made solely of wood, no metal edges and no fittings for boots. A leather length nailed to the sides was strapped across the ski to hold the toe of the boot in place on the ski. Of course, all one had to do was lift a foot and out came the boot. We used jar rubbers made for canning to supplement the strap, first putting our boots through the strap, then pulling the jar rubber back under the toe of the boot to the strap, and then around the back of the boot to stretch over our heels. This held us on to the ski and gave much better control, especially on turns. For poles, we used sticks or scrap lumber. Ski jumps were built of snow on a steep slope, where we iced the sides and surface whenever the temperature allowed. In this way, we built some to a height of eight to ten feet in the air. Sabin's pasture was ideal for this, as the side behind the Seminary sloped sharply to the brook that flowed in the shallow valley at its bottom.

For a short while, the city had a rope tow operated by an old truck motor directly behind the Seminary that drew large crowds of people on weekends. Amazingly, the only real injury I remember in all the time we skied there was when Donald Gross went off the jump one day and fell, breaking his arm and crushing his elbow; a bad break. His arm never fully recovered from this accident, and in later years, although he had some use of the arm, his elbow never allowed the arm to be fully extended. The rest of us had the usual bruises, scratches, and bloody noses, of course, but no injuries that were disabling.

10

Spring, summer, and fall, we used the field in back of the Administration Building of the Seminary for playing baseball and football. As soon as the snow melted off the grass and the field had been dried out by sun and wind, we gathered to choose up teams. The determination of positions was dependent on who brought the ball first, then who brought the bat, as not all of us were fortunate enough to have either. Usually pitcher and first base were awarded to the owners of the ball and bat. Gloves were optional, as some had them but most did not. Catching a ball without a glove resulted in many sprained fingers and hurt palms until we learned the knack of softening the blows by moving our arms back, thus taking up some of the shock. Many rousing games were played with only two or three gloves in evidence. Many hits were made by opposing sides using one bat for all. Innings were not counted, because the only things that ended a game were either mothers calling, sudden rain that stayed, or being evicted by crabby Seminary officials.

Football was played under almost the same rules. Whoever brought a ball got to be captain of his team, and quarterback as well. Sides were chosen by count of kids. For instance, we might start a game five to a side and finish with fourteen a side, depending on when and if more joined in. Everybody played the games, inserted into a position as they showed up. Touch football was not invented at that time, so it was rough, unpadded play, blocking and tackling as hard as we could. There were injuries, such as bloody noses, kicked shins, and so on, but to my knowledge no one was badly hurt. We also played football at two other locations: Emmon's Field at the top of College Street, and the arsenal on College Street across from Dr. Goodwin's house, but these were used only infrequently.

Many days were spent playing these games, and at the approach of twilight, the calls of mothers in the neighborhood would begin to sound. Henry Augustoni's mother would holler "Bambino!"; Arthur Comolli's would blast with "Junior!"; Frank Facini's with "Frankie!" Jim Seivwright's father would bellow "James!"; my mother, "Bobbie!" The hill would echo with a cacophony of hollered voices. We reluctantly would holler back and head for home, another day of sport ended.

The most violent and tragic thing that occurred at one of these games was at Emmon's Field where we were playing football. The Hudsons lived across the street from the field, and Jack Hudson's mother called to him to come home. Jack ignored the call, and soon his brother, Ashley, came to get him. Ashley told Jack to go home right now and Jack said something smart back to him. The next thing we knew, they had started fighting, and before it was over, Ashley had broken Jack's arm. This, of course, broke up the game, and is the only serious injury I can remember of those football days.

Medical care was a world away from what it is today. Doctors made house calls to administer treatment to patients in their own beds. Going to the hospital required an emergency of such proportion that it couldn't be dealt with in the Doctor's office. Arms and legs were set in offices, stitches sewn and open wounds attended there. Being in the hospital was very serious, because that meant, barring operations, that the Doctor had no cure, and you were there to either recover or to pass on, depending only on your immune system and helpful but futile care. Drugs, with the exception of digitalis for heart care, were not in existence at that time. Preferred treatment for pneumonia was Brown's Mixture, an expectorant, and aspirin along with bed care—not very effective at all. The Spanish Flu had claimed millions of lives during the latter part of World War I and the years following. Pneumonia found willing hosts in already weakened systems. It was not until World War II that penicillin and sulfa drugs were perfected to fight infection.

I spent two sessions in the hospital—one for appendicitis and the other for infection from a scrape on my foot at the new swimming pool in 1939. The appendix stay was two weeks in hospital and three weeks of bed rest at home. The infection in my foot was initially treated at home with Epsom Salt soaks and application of Icthamol Ointment to the foot. It did not cure the infection, instead allowing it to spread up my leg to enlarge the glands in my groin. I ended up in hospital where my groin was lanced and drained for many days. My immune system must have come through and saved me, because the infection subsided so I could finally go home.

11

In the thirties, we had things unknown today. Milk was delivered to your door. The milk wagon came at about 4:00 a.m. It was an exciting sight to see coming up the street in pitch darkness. The four corners of the large wagon were mounted with red lanterns that glowed through the mists that swirled in the cool of early morning before the summer sun would evaporate them. The clip-clop of the huge Clydesdale horse hooves advanced ahead of this apparition as it neared the front of my house. I used to love this time of day, as I was usually just starting for my fishing places at that time. It is one of the most pleasant sights and sounds I can recall.

Meat wagons came twice a week—even fruit and vegetables were delivered in each neighborhood weekly. Mr. Cueto and Mr. Parry drove their horse-drawn wagons, covered at the sides and top to preserve the ice that was loaded in before the meat was placed on top. The back had a cutting board that folded down and was braced at the sides so it could act as a chopping block. All the neighborhood women gathered around and selected their meat, while the butchers cut it before their eyes. There was always a large carton of hotdogs and a large tray of ground beef inside the back of the wagon on one side. On the other side was a roll of wrapping paper and string mounted on the inside for packaging. Once in a while, a woman would give her order and then return to her house to get the where-withal to pay for it. Mr. Parry or Mr. Cueto would then cut their order, package it, and proceed to follow the woman to her house to complete the sale. We kids would wait at a distance until this occurred, then swoop like hawks to steal hot-dogs before the butcher returned. You could almost say that we were raised on these scarfed hot dogs and what fruit we could snitch from these vendors.

Autumn with its glory of color, clear blue azure skies, and the hint of frosts to come brought apple pie season. Ripe McIntosh was the preferred base for pur-loined apple pie, and instinct the necessary other ingredient. We knew all the trees in our general vicinity, as well those in other areas. We knew exactly which trees would be ripe at any given time. We were aided by Jim Seivwright's mis-chievous mother, who knew exactly what would spur us on. She often expressed a whimsical yearning for fresh pie, with tongue in cheek. That was all we needed to hear. Armed with borrowed shirts many sizes too large tucked into tightly belted trousers (supplied by Jim's mother and belonging to his father), we would wait until total darkness descended, then leave in a group to forage. Stealthily approaching orchards and individual trees, we would silently pick to fill the shirts, and then leave as quietly as possible. Upon arrival back at Jim's house, his mother would express surprise, mildly castigate us for our thievery, then say that she could not waste our efforts nor the apples, and so she would spend the next two or three days making pies, tarts, and assorted pastries, which we ate with total glee.

We had many adventures in apple stealing. Though sorely tempted, we did not attack in our own immediate neighborhood. I suppose it stemmed from the ethics of "honor among thieves" and a desire not to despoil our own environs. We were also convinced that there were other reasons not to poach so close to home. Mr. Gill, who had a small orchard, along with beehives to produce honey and pollinate the trees, was rumored to have a shotgun loaded with rock salt by his back door, which proved to be an excellent deterrent, whether real or rumor.

Mr. Magne had a large orchard protected by a sheep fence around its perimeters. Within roamed a large German shepherd of unfriendly nature who snarled and barked with ruff raised if you even came close to the fence. The Magnes also had a son, Joe, several years older than us with a magnificent build who was admired and feared, although he was always friendly to us. His immediate neighbors were the Meladas who also had a large, muscular son—a buddy of Joe Magne's—even larger than Joe. The Meladas also had a dog, part shepherd, part wolf, a huge animal who, on moonlit nights, would sit on its haunches and howl at the moon.

The Gales had an apple tree that produced a particularly sweet fruit, probably a Duchess of some variety. This we took an occasional apple from, but did not raid, as they were neighbors. The fruits of many men's labors became our fruits in the true sense of the word. Cherries, plums, and other varieties became our goal quite often. Gardening became hazardous for the upper classes, since we also raided those occasionally. We considered ourselves to be Robin Hoods, distributing our take in our own neighborhood.

One particular heist—the "Up a Tree Incident"—stands tall in my memory. We had spotted a tree situated off Liberty Street growing behind and down the hill from Ed Heney's house on College Street. We knew it belonged to Dr. Martin, Ed's next-door neighbor, who owned property behind his and Ed's house. Dr. Martin had several apple trees directly behind his house, which he guarded jealously during early autumn, but this one was isolated from his orchard by a small stand of high pines. We knew his son Donald was home from college for the weekend. Having calculated this information, we waited until quite late to begin our foray. After watching Donald take out his car and head downtown, we moved in. Jim climbed the tree, which was quite tall, to shake apples down to us on the ground.

Suddenly someone spotted the flashlight heading our way and we skedaddled. That is, all of us on the ground did. Jim was still up the tree. As we watched from a safe distance in our hiding place, we heard voices coming from the area near the tree. Donald Martin had returned and was telling his father that, although we had escaped, he was sure one of us looked like Jim Seivwright. They held a rather long conversation underneath the tree before departing for the house.

It was a good hour before Jim finally joined the rest of us. He explained that before he could jump down from the tree, Don and Dr. Martin had appeared next to it. He said that he could only cling to the branches and hope they would leave before they shone their lights on him in the tree. After being privy to their conversation about Don seeing him run with the rest, plus some very disparaging talk about him in particular, Jim had decided to stay in the tree for that long hour, not taking any more chances. He could hear them talking and thrashing about the main orchard for most of that time, and he didn't know when or if they might return. It was good for many laughs and jokes for some time to come. Had either Don or his father shone their light at the tree itself, they would have spotted Jim for sure.

12

W hen I was a young child, trolleys still served the area. Their tracks ran from the center of Montpelier up East State Street to meet tracks that came up Main Street and down College Street, to Sibley Avenue by way of Sabin Street, then on to Barre Street. Another run of tracks came from Main Street up Barre Street to the Pioneer Bridge. The main line came up State Street to Main, then across the bridge to Northfield Street or turned left up River Street. This line went all the way to Barre where it split—one spur up Washington Street, the other up Main, where it split again to South Main and Ayer Streets. I am sure there were other spurs to serve other areas but I just can't recall them.

As the automobile came in, the trolleys went out. By the time we had moved from Barre to the crowded house on Foster Street, the trolleys no longer ran but the tracks were still embedded all over town, including the main streets.

Both the Barre and Montpelier main downtown areas were cobbled with granite for many years of my childhood. There had been some street paving, but only the main ones. For instance, Barre, Main, East State, Elm, and Liberty Streets, and a few streets that intersected them were paved with a spray of hot tar over a macadam-type base. Most of the smaller streets were still paved with granite dust over either gravel or earth. Foster Street was one of these, giving us the advantage of being able to dig out holes for marble playing or stone bases for our ongoing baseball games. We used the street, for the most part devoid of traffic, for field hockey, with sticks, a stone for a puck, and those holes we had made as goals. Of course, this practice was frowned upon by the authorities—our parents and city officials.

The streets became a menace when dried on hot summer days to dusty particulate. Blown by a rare passing truck or car or by gusts of finicky wind, the granite dust would waft over clean, newly hung clothes, carefully placed on lines just moments before. Also on high wind days, this cloud would blow through open screened windows to grace highly polished tables and stuffed furniture within.

Back roads were another story, most not even graveled. They consisted of dirt alone, which presented the problem of mud, for which Vermont was famous. Even those built of stone and gravel macadam wilted in heavy rains and snowmelt, causing flood conditions. The gravel and stone became one with the earth below to produce prolific ooze, in mud season and out.

I can recall the first paving, by concrete section, of the Barre-Montpelier Road. After the initial roadwork of gravel was up to grade, the surface was laid out by small flags, with string set on stakes, the large sections of one side of the proposed road boxed in with wooden sides. Extruded steel lay in a grid within, raised to a height of half the depth to be concreted, and tied in by wire ties. Then concrete, mixed on the job, was poured into the forms and leveled to the top. Then the process was repeated up the road. The other side was started, eventually catching up with the paving of that particular section. In this way, and with cooperation of summer weather, the whole distance was eventually covered, but not in one season.

Soon after the paving of the Barre-Montpelier road, buses were introduced by Vermont Transit, running between the two communities, traveling from Taylor Street in Montpelier to Depot Square in Barre. For ten cents, you could catch the bus by merely standing beside the route and waving it to a stop or by showing up at the terminals for the full ride. These terminals were located in the train stations of each town.

This enabled me to see my relatives in Barre about once a month. I could catch the bus by crossing the Granite Street Bridge and wait at the store, which was in the apex of the V formed by the connection of River and Berlin Streets. I would give my ten cents to the driver, take a seat and get off at Depot Square, then walk to my Grandmother's house on Keith Avenue. Sometimes Mother would call ahead so that Uncle Cecil could meet me at Depot Square. I would spend the day, usually a Saturday, with my Grandmother and Uncle Cecil, then return to Montpelier in the early evening.

I could always tell where I was on the ride by the bumps I was going over. The older buses had springs, but not shock absorbers, so I felt every bump acutely. On cobbles, it was a short jerky motion up and down, emphasized by the slower speed we were going in town. The open roadway was somewhat smoother—that is, between the concrete sections. Of course, when the bus ran over the sections and hit the cracks between, we experienced a sharp bounce and a clunk would sound through the tires, acting much like the action of a train rolling over joints in the rails. In the spring, this was exaggerated by the frost having heaved sections at different levels, so that the ride was even bumpier.

On cold days in winter, the primitive heaters of the time kept the driver warm but hardly penetrated the vast interior of the bus, particularly in the back where deeply frosted windows were common. On days of heavy snow, chains were put on at one of the terminals. This made for a rougher, if safer, tractioned ride. Usually one or two links in the chains would break loose, giving a clunk-rattle where they struck the fenders on each wheel rotation. A chatter from the chains striking the pavement as the wheel rotated could be felt in the seats.

In those days, carsickness was a constant problem for me, and the rougher ride only exacerbated my nausea. Motion sickness with me was a given whenever I rode in a car or train, and even when I tried, with the other kids, to play on the swings. Whether it was brought on by my frequent earaches caused by infections or was just a simple problem of inner ear imbalance, I do not know. I just know I dreaded car rides and, in defense, tried to sleep through them.

These trips to Barre were most enjoyable for me since they were the only time that anyone paid much attention to me. Cecil became my surrogate father and we did many things together. He took me to see Tom Mix, the great western star of movie fame, and finagled me close enough to shake Tom's hand personally at a promotional for his latest picture. In those times, movie stars had to promote their own movies all over the country. Tom Mix came to Barre in a Duesenberg touring car with a convertible top that was as long by half again as the usual car of the day. High-set headlights and a V-shaped grill gleamed in chrome plate. Super chargers in luminous chrome sprouted from each front side, giving the impression of tremendous power. The spare tires fit in a scooped-out area in back of the front fenders, which flared on either side to the long running boards and on to the back fender. These enclosed the bulky square trunk, which hung at the back of this huge boat-like apparition.

Used to seeing dainty Model-T or Model-A Fords, or square, squat, bulky Hudsons and Oldsmobiles, this was a stunning sight to my eyes. The main color was a brilliant red, with cream-colored leather upholstery, the epitome of class and style. Crowds of both children and adults lined the main street of Barre from Depot Square to the park as he slowly drove up from the Paramount Theater to the Opera House. Cecil's pure bulk, combined with his audacity, got us right up to the driver's side of the car where he held me up to shake Tom's hand. It was a great thrill.

I also got to see Richard Dix, and Laurel and Hardy, and to shake their hands. Cecil usually took me to the matinee at either the Opera House or the Paramount Theater, where he loaded me with peanuts and candy for the feature film. After the movies, we would make the rounds of his close friends who were in business in Barre—Mar's tobacco shop, Angelo's restaurant, where we would sit for coffee (soda for me) and chat with Angelo, Bill Sykas' pool room, and so on—returning to Grandmother's until bus time came. I always enjoyed being spoiled by him, if only for an occasional day.

Grandmother Webster would make much of me on those visits, praising my growth and inquiring about my schooling in a maternal way. She would usually have dinner at noon on the days I visited, cooking my favorites of either steak, fin 'n haddie, or lamb patties with small early June peas and potatoes. I always enjoyed her thick Scottish brogue as she told me tales of the "old days." We rarely discussed family except when I would bring up my namesake Bert, short for Robert, who was killed in World War I in France. Then this greatest of treasures would light up her eyes and she would proceed to tell me about her life as a Gold Star Mother.

In World War I, most of the slain were laid to rest in French cemeteries near their combat zones. After the Great War ended, as an expression of compassion the government paid to send the Gold Star Mothers by ship to France to visit these graves. This seems to have been the highlight of Grandmother's life. When telling me her story, she would become more animated, almost joyful, as she told me of her trip. It seems that Bert was killed by shellfire in the trenches in the Forest of the Ardennes, and all the gory details, imagined or true, were related over and over to me. Her trip to France was also related in great detail, especially the graveyard scene and the government ceremony at graveside. I could never match her enthusiasm on this subject. Whenever I tried to pry other family history from her, it was with great reluctance that she would talk at all about her Scotland experiences, and I can only conclude that it was not a happy time in her life.

I did drag out of her bits of information, such as the origins of her maiden name, Chalmers. The name was taken during the time when Camerons were shipped to France to fight alongside their French Army, becoming known to the French Court as fierce fighters. Their leaders were given the name Chalmers, which stuck long after their return to their native Scotland where they again joined the Camerons. She and my grandfather left Scotland from Huntley, the seat of the Gordon clan where the name Webster abounds. Huntley is located in the extreme north of Aberdeenshire on Scotland's eastern coast. Grandmother Webster died while I was in the army in Japan, and I've always regretted that I never pressed her for more pertinent information.

These little interludes imbued me with a sense of family that I never really felt with the Ewen side. Mostly they were kind to me, but I never sensed that I belonged to them. At that time, divorce was not altogether rare, but of all my companions, I happened to be the only one with divorced parents. The bitter feelings of my mother toward my father, even though much deserved, palled my relationship with her and her family, and led to feelings of inadequacy in myself that I had to combat for many years. The expression "you're just like your father" piqued these feelings until I was old enough to rationalize that I was not like my father at all.

13

In my early adolescence, hitching posts still stood in front of most merchants' stores set between the cobbled streets and the granite dust sidewalks. In both Barre and Montpelier granite watering troughs completed the picture. Saturday's horse drawn vehicles outnumbered the automobiles parked along the main thoroughfares of the towns in our area, and the bibbed overalls outnumbered the dress suits. Even when the gradual changes came, such as the closing of the trolley lines and more autos in town, the horse drawn wagons still could be seen, especially on Saturday, market day, in some numbers.

The one man whose presence impressed me the most was Mr. Clark, from Shady Rill, a rural community lying off the road from Montpelier to Worcester. Between the hours of 8:00 a.m. and 9:00 a.m., he would arrive in town, his high-stepping black mare drawing his light, black wagon trimmed with red painted spokes on all four wheels, and leather appointed seat. The tailgate and sides were painted with bold white letters spelling out "Jesus Saves".

Perched stiff-backed on the wagon seat, his imposing figure was dressed in a clean black suit graced with a stark white celluloid collar on an immaculate shirt that was partially covered by a light brown vest. A chain draped across the vest, to which was attached his pocket watch of some dimension. Topping his stately head was a light gray Stetson, rarely seen in Eastern States. Across his Roman nose spanned a pair of pince-nez glasses. Underneath this prominence a black mustache in the style of Teddy Roosevelt graced his upper lip.

In the wagon bed were bushel baskets of vegetables from his large garden. His clean and ordered appearance and his horse's shining harness, along with the spotless wagon he drew, stood out in comparison to all the other dingy and dirt-streaked wagons that would arrive later in the day. The quality of his produce was evident in its fresh-washed look, and the size of such vegetables as cabbage, lettuce and carrots put other farmers to shame.

As he stepped from his wagon perch to the cobbles of Main Street and paced to tie his horse to the hitching rail, his well-polished high-heeled boots gleamed in the early morning sun. Tall and straight-backed, he stood next to his horse, awaiting his repeat customers. He always watered the horse shortly after arrival, and fitted it with an oat-filled feedbag over the horse's muzzle before making his first sale.

I would watch from a short distance as he plied his wares with superb dignity and calm demeanor. Customers flocked to his wagon bed, exchanging conversation. He carefully placing the money he collected into a large leather pouch that somehow appeared from a jacket pocket. His age, to me, was indeterminate, his bearing regal, and I imagined him to be a hero of the Spanish-American War, a "Rough Rider" who had charged up San Juan Hill.

By noon of a Saturday, he would have sold his produce and headed back up Main Street on his way back home. For many years, I watched this spectacle and never saw it vary, even when Friday night shopping replaced Saturday. Although the cobbled streets were paved and the horse troughs and hitches removed, on any Saturday morning well into the late 1940's, Mr. Clark regularly appeared.

Some years later, I became acquainted with his only child, a daughter, who became a faithful customer of mine. When asked about her father, she proudly answered that yes, indeed, he had fought in that war and had been an ardent admirer of Teddy Roosevelt. He had also been a deeply religious man. My imagination had been correct and my admiration of this seemingly strange man rose even higher.

14

Automobiles were a rarity in our neighborhood, due, I am sure, to the effects of the Great Depression. Very few people could afford them. Guido Magne had a second-hand Ford sedan, with a square, box-like body with running boards on either side as wide as the fenders over each wheel. These tapered in the front to frame the long hood which, when opened by unlatching and lifting a side, revealed a solid block engine. The engine consisted of a cast iron block with a few wires running to a battery, then on to the so-called firewall, then through this to the steering column. A small lever, situated just under the wheel, controlled the settings on a magneto wire to the battery. When starting the engine, you adjusted this lever to start position, turned the key on the dash, and pressed a starter button situated next to the keyhole. If you were lucky, the car started.

However, in cold weather, and even sometimes on damp days, the battery did not kick the starter over. You had to get out and, with a crank made to fit a hole in the car front under the grill, crank the motor to turn it over. It took a technique of combined strength and rhythm to do it right, with a quick down-stroke and a snap on the up-stroke. The engine would fire and race while you ran back to the driver's cab to adjust the magneto to idle. The engine had direct mounts to the frame of the car, so when it started, the entire body shook as the engine raced. Only fine adjustment to the magneto calmed it down. Once started, you released the hand brake, applied pressure to the gas pedal, and moved onto the road. Any let-up on the gas pedal slowed the car measurably on a flat road, so the very action of driving was a physical challenge as well as mechanical. Your right leg was constantly applying pressure, causing it to become quite tired on a long drive. The brakes, when applied, only braked on two wheels, resulting in many skids that had to be manhandled with the wheel, which also was tiring. Only the light-weight of the vehicle enabled any real control.

The horn was an actual horn-shaped metal cylinder in front of the driver, mounted on the firewall and controlled by a large button in the middle of the steering wheel. When compressed by the driver, a sharp sound emanated from the horn and, when held down, produced the sound of the times, "Aururaaa!" which could not fail to get your attention.

The tires, which were much smaller in circumference than today's, being about five inches in diameter, were made of rubber and inflated with an inner tube much like a bicycle tire. They were hand pumped by a pump also used to inflate bicycle tires and footballs. They gave little cushion to road shocks when combined with the inadequate leaf springs of the day. Every little or large bump in the road was directly transmitted to the passengers of the vehicle, since the seats were merely padded over a series of coil springs bolted to the floor. Seat backs did not tilt at all, but stiffly held your back upright, which put all your weight on your buttocks to catch the bumps and jiggles of the road.

The car had a one-speed window wiper that kept the driver's side of the windshield somewhat clear, but on snowy days it clogged, and the car had to be stopped so the blade could be cleared frequently. Tire chains were used on snow-covered roads or icy surfaces. We had to find chains to fit the back wheels and during storms they had to be laid out, then driven on. Next you had to reach for the ends, which had latches to close, fasten them together, and hope they stayed on. This also added to the bumps, although it also added greatly to the traction of the tires.

A steel bumper was bolted to both front and back to protect the body of the car in the event of an accident. It also came into play when the car got stuck either in mud or snow, providing a sturdy platform to push against or to attach a chain or rope. Many cars were put back on the road by being pulled from mire by horses belonging to farmers. If all else failed, several men could take hold of a bumper and physically lift the car out. Model-A Fords were very light, and could usually be pushed by one man while the driver maneuvered the car.

Guido Magne had devised a boat rack from pieces of pipe that formed a frame over the body of his car and attached to the running boards at its corners. It held a homemade plywood boat which weighed about 60-70 pounds that could be hoisted by two men on to the rack, then tied down with straps. He had a one and a half horsepower Johnson outboard motor that powered the boat very well, especially at trolling speed. With this rig, he and members of the neighborhood fished most of the lakes and ponds of northern Vermont in the late 30's and early 40's.

The Model-A also became the neighborhood's hunting vehicle when the season rolled around. The memories of being packed into what was essentially a four-seater car, dressed in heavy woolen clothing ready for snow or rain, with three or four other people and two to three wet dogs for the long ride back home from a hunt fill me with conflicting pleasure and relief. The smells as we traveled home would peak about mid-ride, as body heat built in men and dogs until they reached gagging proportions. Windows would be rolled down for breaths of fresh air, and then swiftly closed as the cold penetrated every fiber of our being. Inevitably, somewhere down the road, either man or beast would expel exceedingly pungent air to add to the heavy fragrance within the car. Windows would swiftly go down with appropriate comment until the air stabilized, then go back up to hold the meager warmth. Feet would be leaden with cold on the thin metal floors, and much stomping would add to the tumult of sounds of coughing, swearing, dog whining and the putt-putt-putt of the car's motor. Guns, held by those in the back seat, would butt into thighs or shins after a few miles on the road and have to be rearranged frequently.

But all in all, there would be the pleasant memories of the day's hunt to ponder in your mind. Reliving comic doings, such as someone falling from a perch on top of a brush pile, breaking through the ice of a stream crossed, or shots missed because of surprise, would be discussed repeatedly and appropriately laughed about. Camaraderie would be at its peak, and good healthy ribbing would keep us in stitches for many miles. Toward the end of the drive, fatigue would take over and long silences would ensue. Cleaning the game upon arrival home would be groaned about, and the morrow's workday would become uppermost in our minds. My thoughts would be on clean up and a hot bath to prepare for the upcoming school day. Sadness would prevail as we approached the home limits of the neighborhood, all of us sensing that perhaps we now had to pay for our pleasure.

On one of these forays, we had decided to hunt around Joe's Pond in West Danville, a drive of some distance on a cold winter's day. In the hurry to get ready, I had discovered that my high-cuts had not dried since building an igloo the previous day. The only other boots I had at the time were a castoff pair of ski boots, which covered just above my ankles. I hurried to dress and laced them on my wool-socked feet, not even noticing at the time that the heavy wool socks were a little too tight.

On reaching the area we were to hunt, we parked by a gate leading to a road in a vast forest of spruce. We crossed the gate, and immediately the dogs commenced to howl that they had started a hare. Hurrying up the wood trail, we crossed a swamp of some size in which I promptly went over my ski boots into icy cold, swampy water. Stupidly, I kept on trying to ignore the socks, now saturated, cold and wet in my boots. As long as I was moving, it wasn't too bad, but as the day progressed, I had to stand still at times as the dogs drove rabbits by. The temperature dropped rapidly until I became aware of my ears and nose tip coming to a perfect freeze. The ice, which now clung to my exposed socks, acutely reminded me that my feet were beginning to freeze. All I could do when I stepped was hope my foot would come down where I had aimed it, because I could not feel my feet strike the ground.

I quit hunting and rather gingerly returned to the car, which by this time would have made an excellent refrigerator. I tried to stomp some circulation into my feet, but was not rewarded by any return of feeling for my effort. Knowing I was in real trouble, I spotted a farmhouse across the road and perhaps half a mile in the distance. Shaking and shivering, I stumbled on those leaden stubs in frozen boots to the farmhouse and knocked on the door.

It finally opened to reveal an old woman in a housedress and apron who quickly appraised my condition and prompted me to come in. She led me to a typical farm kitchen and placed a chair directly in front of the huge cast iron stove that was radiating heat to the whole room. I unlaced my boots and, with some difficulty, removed them, along with my socks, to find two pale white feet. She placed an agate pan in front of me and proceeded to fill it with hot water from a huge kettle on the stove. After some mixture with cooler water, she rolled up my unlaced Johnson pants and placed my feet in the pan. Agony knew no bounds, as the hot water seemed to boil my feet, bringing unabashed tears streaming down my cheeks. To take my mind off my pain, she kept a running conversation going, all the while moving about the kitchen preparing hot tea. When she handed me a cup, it was so hot I could barely keep my hands on it. They too had become frostbitten and were white in color.

Finally, the warmth of the water in the agate pan, the roaring stove, and the hot tea penetrated enough to relax me somewhat, and I could begin to answer her rapid questions. After hearing me explain what had happened and why, she replied in a rich Scottish brogue that my hunting partners and I were damned fools. I proceeded to get a long discourse on common sense and how to use it. She was right, of course, and I had to agree with her about it. After a while, she calmed down and asked where I was from. I answered by giving her my name and address in Montpelier. Upon hearing my last name, she inquired of the Webster side, and as I told her, she began to smile. It seems she knew my grandmother, having been with her on the Gold Star trip to France. She also knew Uncle Cecil through Clan Gordon functions in Barre. I spent a pleasant couple of hours sipping the strongest tea I ever drank, talking about many things, foremost of which was my common ancestry with hers. In that short span of time, she had changed for me from a dour, no-nonsense farmer's wife to a typical Gaelic old lady, warm and gregarious.

My boots, though hardened, had dried somewhat, and my socks had dried thoroughly in the oven of the huge stove. I placed them on my feet, thoroughly warm at last. I thanked her profusely again and made my way to the car where the others were just arriving. I told them my story and we left for home.

I can't help but marvel, even today, at having found myself at that particular farmhouse with that particular woman when I needed it most. One small carelessness could have resulted in catastrophe were it not for that bit of luck. Without her intervention, I am convinced that I would have sustained long lasting and disastrous injury. I never repeated the stupidity of wearing the wrong boots again.

15

Occasionally (too often for my taste) my mother, grandmother, or one of my many aunts would be inspired by religious fervor and would start going to church. I am sure my rebellious nature had been noted. I would be washed, clean clothed, and shipped off to Sunday school while they attended church services. These periods, however, were somewhat brief, as their zeal diminished into boredom after so many weeks of faithful attendance.

Though I disliked going to Sunday school, it did have little benefits. I learned that there were differences between good and evil, though it seemed to me that these depended on who you were, not what you were doing, and I suppose that my exposure, however brief, did allow some teachings to stick. Usually sometime during our classes on fundamental religion, cookies or some sort of pastry would be served, and palm leaf branches distributed to us. Much of that sort of thing was lost on me, particularly on a sunny Sunday morning. These interludes were short, for which I thanked that God or Jesus about which I was supposed to be learning. I soon went back to my heathen ways on Sundays—fishing, ball playing, or just plain doing nothing.

When Father Knapp of the Episcopal Church recruited boys for his church choir, Frank Facini, Jr. and I joined others every Thursday night for choir practice, and Sunday morning sang in the choir. Our motivation was the ten cents paid at every meeting, including practice. It became quite lucrative, and we soon fulfilled demands for other church services in the area as well. All this went well for a few years, until some bright church deacon passed a resolution that we not be paid to perform. The whole system collapsed. This helped to steady my belief that, although one was expected to give generously to whatever church, one was not to ask for it to be given to him.

When not being harried at church, school or work, or lacking enough friends for a ball game, or having fished the day before—or for whatever reason—time could lay heavy on our hands. During these times we made use of our backs. That is, we laid on them in a field or lawn and simply watched the clouds. Conversation was low key. You could point out a particular formation which in your sight or imagination resembled something—Indian heads, angels, dogs, cats, even ships at sea—as the clouds slowly churned across an otherwise deep blue sky. Gossip or animated conversation was more or less taboo, unless you sat up to tell it. Quiet hours were passed in this endeavor with an occasional comment breaking through the warm sunshine or lazy thought.

Grown-ups and otherwise ambitious people called this "doing nothing." This seemed to bother some adults, who, upon spying us in our labors, arrived to employ our talents elsewhere. We, however, considered ourselves to be gainfully employed in a learning process. Our thoughts, between watching unusual clouds, would be on deep blue space. We wondered what was up there and if there really was infinity. Certainly our minds would tell us there had to be boundaries of some sort to that blue, and we were right, of course. We would rarely express these thoughts to others, but on occasion would, if prompted, expound on our theories.

We would spy highflying hawks or flights of what we supposed were larks in the sky and follow their mastery of flight with undivided attention. We all wanted to be up there with them in their seemingly effortless spiraling. Then some parent would call for one of us and our reverie would be broken, our day of leisure at an end. We would go our separate ways back into the world of lawn mowing, garbage removal, lawn raking, errand running, or to other innumerable tasks. The sky would still be blue and the clouds still pool across it, but it wasn't just ours anymore.

Most of the time, when something wasn't planned ahead, we wandered in pairs or groups. I hesitate to say gangs. We considered ourselves loosely allied, but individual in our motives. If we met another individual, pair or group alien or antagonistic to us, and one of us had a grievance with another, we fought our own battles. Our friends were perhaps morally supportive, but stood neutral to the other's fray.

Usually we would group up for the Saturday afternoon matinee at the Strand Theater on Main Street, which always showed the latest B western flicks. Those were the days of Gene Autry, Lash LaRue, Tom Mix, Richard Dix, Hopalong Cassidy, Buck Jones, and newcomers Roy Rogers and Dale Evans. Serials were also run before the feature film. These were shown in segments each week, always ending in an impossible situation for the hero, such as hanging by a branch over a high cliff with the branch pulling out of the rock cleft it had grown in. Of course, the next week he escaped certain death by some miraculous means. These kept your interest and ensured your presence for next week's segment.

Other series usually consisted of a hero and a villain, and were famous radio show or comic strip characters such as the Green Hornet, the Shadow, the Spider, the Lone Ranger, Buck Rogers, Tarzan, some evil villain, or animal trainers like Buck Jones and Clyde Beatty. Some of these characters became vivid in our imaginations and we tried to emulate the heroes in our daily play, wearing bed sheet capes and brandishing homemade swords, spears, knives, and guns, all made of wood scraps. We even tried to mimic the steeds of the famed characters, such as Blaze, Midnight, Champion, Silver, and Trigger. We would run with a kind of skip-leap to catch the motion of a horse whenever we were running. In our imaginations, we became those sturdy steeds. Sabin's pasture, with its rolling hills and gullies, was perfect for such play, and we spent numerous hours racing up and down its slopes.

Finding our favorite seat would be our first order of business for an afternoon at the theater, usually with most of the other kids in the balcony waiting for the lights to darken, sitting through a short feature, a newsreel, then on to the serial, after which there was a short intermission. This enabled us to relieve ourselves in the highly odiferous rest rooms, buy more popcorn or candy (if we could afford to), and return to our seats. The lights would dim again and the feature would begin. Sometimes the film would break in the projection room and the lights would come back on while the projectionist either fixed the film or re-threaded it through the sprockets it had jumped out of when it stopped showing. This was cause for hollering and stamping of feet from anxious kids. Old Mr. Gill who ran the theater would proceed to the stage and shout us down with dire warnings of expulsion. Most would quiet down and wait patiently for the repairs to be made and, with rare exception, the lights would soon dim and the film would roll on. However, sometimes it would skip that portion you had been watching and break the continuity of the plot. Still, we would watch with renewed fascination for the rest of the show. Then, of course, there were the times the projectionist would show reels out of order and all the above would apply.

There was one other theater in Montpelier at that time, but we never went to it because it only played sophisticated films like love stories, which held little interest for us. It was not until we were in high school that we started attending the Capitol Theater. I remember my first viewing there of a film based in a tropical location where the main plot was built around a romance in the middle of a vicious hurricane. *Hurricane* was, by the way, the name of the picture, and though I can't remember the actors or actresses by name, I was properly impressed with the staging and plot, as well as the photography, since it was the first color film I had ever seen. It was also my first class A film.

16

The early 1930's, even though it was during the Depression with its labor strife, and monetary hardship, had their moments of relief and elation. The spotting of a rare aeroplane, or airplane as they came to be called (they were aer-o-planes to us), was cause for alerting the whole neighborhood. I recall one day hearing a motor on the horizon and spotting what turned out to be a Beech craft bi-wing painted scarlet red coming over our street end to end.

Hollering "Airplane, airplane!" I rushed to the house where every-one—Grandmother, aunts, cousins—spilled out onto the street. Neighbors, alerted by my cries and the repeated cries of their various kids, rushed to the center of the street to see this phenomenon pass over us all with a classic roar of its powerful engine and a gentle waggle of its wing by the pilot. The whole neighborhood, with few exceptions, was milling about the street, talking excitedly.

Another time an airship—a dirigible—albeit not large, silently followed the Winooski River Valley heading, we supposed, to the Barre Fairgrounds where they were having some sort of to-do at the time. It was not until the advent of World War II that the sight of aircraft of any kind solicited casual observance rather than high excitement from the beholder. Even then, the sighting of high flying military aircraft still brought people out of their homes.

I recall only one or two barnstorming aircraft shows at the old Barre-Montpelier airport in the latter part of the 30's or early 40's. These consisted mostly of bi-wing planes, with an occasional Piper Cub single-wing thrown into the group. The bi-planes ranged from World War I Curtis fighters with no armament to Beech craft or Stillmans, with an occasional Fokker, a World War I German plane. They would do barrel rolls, loops and turns, either singly or with another plane to simulate combat tactics found in the Great War.

Rides were given to those with coin in hand. Once Cecil paid to have me take my first flight in a Stearman bi-plane, strapped securely in the open cockpit, goggled and scarfed, as well as scared silly. We took off, climbed over the airport, did a slow bank over the Barre-Montpelier road, and landed. It was a great thrill, exceedingly short, but memorable in the extreme. I think the fee was a dollar and a half, which at that time was considerable. I am forever grateful to have had an uncle to take over for my father and allow me opportunities such as this that I would not have had otherwise.

Wing walkers were a popular attraction, where a person (usually female) clothed in a white outfit complete with leather helmet and goggles would leave the open cockpit, step onto the wing of the flying aircraft, walk between the struts supporting the two wings, and station him or herself in straps attached to the wing and struts. The pilot would then put the aircraft through loops and rolls and stalls while the walker held on for dear life. The walker would pretend to slip occasionally and, while everyone held their breath, would right to the former position, to the extreme relief and thunderous applause of the spectators. Accidents did happen, according to radio and newspaper reports, and usually death for the wing walker was the result of their daring-do gone wrong. I never witnessed any of these accidents, but was as enthralled as everyone else was by their act.

Once at one of these shows a wing walker who looked quite bulky seemed to fall off the wing. Everyone looked with awe as she plummeted toward the earth. Suddenly, a parachute popped out behind her and she swung suspended, rocking gently to and fro until she landed on the grassy portion of the airfield. It had all been planned, but was unexpected by the crowd, who showed their relief expressively. It was the highlight of the show. Never for a second did I think the incident portended my future. Little did I know.

17

Telephones in the early 1930's were becoming more modern, in that you no longer had to ring in to the operator. Newer phones at that time were made so that, by merely picking up the receiver, contact would automatically be established with the operator's switchboard. Consequently, the old boxes were being replaced with the new phones.

The telephone company (Ma Bell) had its equipment garage behind the stone sheds by the railroad tracks beyond Barre Street. The old box-type phones were stacked about the yard where they were being stripped of all metal parts to be scrapped. The metal being pulled from the wooden boxes for salvage was the large magnets, and the magnetos, which when cranked produced an electrical charge.

Not being very farsighted, we would sneak down Sabin's pasture, cross Barre Street, follow the rails to the telephone yard, and steal all the magnets and magnetos we could carry and leave the boxes behind. Today these complete sets of old telephones bring high antique prices. Our interest was only in those parts that we could play with.

We used the magnets to pick up bits of metal we found lying around. The magnetos we used as shocking devices, wiring up chairs and other things so as to surprise unsuspecting victims. The charge generated by cranking the motors of the magnetos was mild and, although shocking, did no harm to the recipients of our malice. Intense maneuvering was necessary to get our victims placed in unsuspecting contact.

Shelley Miller, Fuzz Taylor, Pete Sykas and I would attach wires to a chair and, while the others kept the attention of each victim, one of us would slip quietly to the crank, give it a few quick turns, and watch the certain reaction of our prey. This worked quite well for some time, until Shelley's father found us out. We were summarily told to dismantle the device immediately. Adults always seemed to spoil our fun.

We became very familiar with the fauna of the field, swamps, and woods. Birds became a source of interest, particularly when observing their nests. We would find them, watch for the eggs, and follow their hatching and feeding until they left their nests. It was great fun to observe them in this way, always being careful not to disturb the parents.

Reptiles such as garter snakes and frogs were not treated with the respect shown birds. On finding snakes or frogs of suitable size and quantity, we would capture them in large cans or jars for later disposal at the Seminary Halls. Sometime after gloaming and before the dormitory doors were locked, we would sneak up, open the doors quietly, and release our charges inside. We would then repair to vantage points where we could see and hear reactions while hidden from view. After a usual wait of a half hour, shrieks would be heard and doors would open to emit variously clad girls all aflutter. The state of terror invoked by our deed gave us great pleasure for some time after we melted away, long before the janitorial staff could start a search.

18

Jogging and running today are generally accepted to be a healthful pastime. In my youth, walking, or shanks-mare, was the common mode of transportation even for adults. Most everyone walked to school or work without a second thought. Where there were sidewalks, pairs, trios, and even foursomes walked in animated conversation. Where there were not, streets would be covered with groups of people going or coming from school or work. Even into the 50's, people on their noon hour lunch breaks filled the downtown sidewalks in Montpelier. East State Street would be surrounded by people on sidewalks as they walked home for lunch and returned to work. Cars usually were used only on weekends for recreation or to visit relatives. Weekday parking was not the problem it is today, and after 5:00 p.m. the main streets were all but deserted.

Western movies influenced me with their constant action, and from the age of about ten years until the age of fourteen, I ran whenever I could. Even when going fishing, I ran to my destination and back home after the day. My favorite run started at home, went up to the college campus, to Sabin's pasture, down to the brook, then up beside the slate quarry and into the woods beyond. I scarcely slowed through the woods onto the Montpelier Country Club where I crossed its uppermost fairways, and made the return trip in reverse order. I would be home in time to meet with the other kids for games. The feel of the wind on the sides of my face, the feeling of power as I flowed over the ground, and the sights of the day filled me with elation. The time alone gave me relief from the many people in my life. When you live with five or six women, all of whom are concerned that you might shirk from your work, and a brother younger than you, and two cousins, all in constant motion in restricted space, you have little time alone. So I ran everywhere I could and truly enjoyed it. Even at that young age, I abhorred wasting time and this filled many hours.

When I was much younger, I had worked at odd jobs in the neighborhood, most of them non-paying, as they were merely neighborly reciprocations. I had one paying job every Saturday morning. This was for a Swedish woman by the name of Johnson who lived down our street. My job there consisted of removing the furnace ashes accumulated that week, cleaning up the cellar, burning paper trash in her trash barrel, and setting her garbage out. In winter, I shoveled her walks, and in spring raked her lawn and prepared her small garden for planting. In the summer, I hand-mowed her lawn with its precipitous banks and did whatever chores she had. Believe me, she could find them for me. I usually worked from about eight in the morning until noon, and all for the magnificent sum of ten cents, the price of admission to the theater. There was always a sense of urgency as noon approached because I was on a tight schedule. The matinee started at 1:15 p.m. and I had to clean myself up, change clothes, eat, and then race for the theater. It always seemed that she deliberately found one more chore to do as noon approached, almost as if to ensure that she got her money's worth out of me.

Mr. Tabor, whose house faced College Street, had a large lot that went down College to Foster Street. It covered all the land on the upper side of Foster bordered by Edwards Street, which paralleled College. It had a steep bank on the Foster Street side of perhaps fifteen feet, where it more or less leveled with the height of his driveway. We were allowed to play on the end bordering Edwards Street, but not on the half bordering College. Mr. Tabor was a tall thin man, evidently retired at this time. He seemed quite dour and we feared him, so we respected his wishes by keeping off the forbidden portion of his land. It was not until I had entered high school and no longer used his field that I got to know him.

When girls, clothes to improve my appearance, and the means to support both started becoming important to me, I went from house to house all over Seminary Hill offering to mow lawns, rake, spade, or clean up things in general. When I got to Mr. Tabor's house, I was quite apprehensive because of his reputation in the neighborhood. I knocked on his back door, and when he opened it, I explained what I was up to, all the while very nervous and expecting some sharp remark. He listened as I explained that I was looking for work and would be willing to do whatever he wished me to do. He smiled, opened the door wider and asked me to come in. We sat at his kitchen table and he proposed what I could do for him, which included mowing his lawn, cleaning out his garden areas, helping him prune bushes and trees, and other yard work. No wages were discussed at this time, although he gave me assurance that he would pay what I was worth. I accepted. He said to be there at 8:00 a.m. on Saturday.

Saturday morning quickly came and I was at his house at eight o'clock sharp. I worked until noon, took a quick lunch break, and returned at 12:30, continuing until about 5:00 p.m. He said he had two more small jobs and asked if I would be available Monday afternoon after school. As we were in solid session going to school from 7:45 a.m. to 1:00 p.m., I said yes. I returned on Monday about 2:00

p.m., and the two of us finished these chores by about four o'clock. It was a warm fall day in early September, and after we finished we had lemonade and sat on his back porch talking—that is, I listened as he talked about his life and family with good humor. He had grown up on a farm, spent most of his life there, and in later years had worked for the State of Vermont Agriculture Department. He had an ancestral relative who had been one of the richest men in the world in the 1800's. This man had owned the Comstock Lode at the time of its earliest and greatest production. He had built mansions there and in New York, had fêted the socially rich of the era and, through a series of unfortunate investments, died a pauper. We talked almost until dark.

As I got up to go home, he handed me an envelope containing my pay. When I got home, I opened it and found it contained $7.00, a large sum for that time, since wages were only fifteen to twenty dollars a week. After that, I worked for him all through high school and spent many happy hours with him in conversation. I found out that, far from being a crabby old man, he was a pleasant person who, with little effort, I could get to know and enjoy. I learned the valuable lesson that appearances are deceiving and not to judge by them.

19

Sugaring was a special time for everybody in Vermont in those days, not the least our bunch. We had by that time of year become bored with winter sports and with the dreary weather. There was always that hint in the air of an unexpected scent of coming spring and welcome warmth. The snows of winter were gradually melting back to allow glimpses of light brown grasses in fields of solid white. It was an awakening of the spirit for us, and we would doff our deep winter gear, somewhat early according to the adults, put on lighter clothing, and run on those grasses that now showed. Our destination was the Phillips farm on Towne Hill Road, reached by cutting across Sabin's pasture to the woods beyond.

We would check each bucket on the maples for sap, and when we found one without the usual dead moths and insects, we would drink some to test for sweetness. Sometimes we even mustered our courage and went to the sugarhouse in hopes of getting a spoonful of syrup. There was something special about those days—clear skies, warm sun and hope of real spring to come.

As we were returning from the sugarbush on one of these forays, one of us spied another early visitor—a skunk. With proper respect and distance, we hied it on its way until it ducked into a stonewall. It kept poking its head out, and once started out to run away. The amazing thing is that it didn't spray us during the entire performance. As it stuck its head out the next time, one of us, I can't remember who, threw a large rock, which hit it right on the head, killing it, whereupon it released its heady fume. There had to have been seven or eight of us milling around at the time, including Bobby Magne and my brother Donald. They were younger than the rest of us, and we, of course, ignored them as they tagged along after us.

The excitement of the chase being over, we continued on our way home, only to be sidetracked on Summit Street where Mr. Gill was trying to untangle a swarm of his bees from the branch of an apple tree. We were fascinated and stopped to watch. He was dressed in his beekeeper's outfit, with a wide-brimmed hat covered with netting, long gloves, loose fitting wool pants, and high rubber boots. In his left hand, he held his smoker, from which clouds of smoke arose. By soothing the swarm with the smoke, he used his right hand to search for the Queen bee at the center of the ball formed by the swarm.

As we were intently watching him, someone noticed Bobby Magne and my brother coming from College Street behind us. There was Donald, tears streaking his dirty face, with the dead skunk cradled in his arms. We rushed over to him and tried to talk him into releasing the skunk, but to no avail. Somebody tried to pry it from him but he wouldn't let go. All we could do was follow him down the hill home. On his arrival there, he went around to the back porch, where he gently laid the skunk down and headed in the door to the kitchen.

After a brief moment, a commotion burst through the open door. Out came Donald, followed by Aunt Edith, with her hands on his shoulders, steering him out before her. Her nose was held high and was wrinkled back, her mouth wide open, gasping. She was followed by assorted other aunts in the same posture, who were hauling out the copper canning tub used as a bathtub for small children, and jars of canned tomatoes. Donald was stripped, doused with the juice from the tomatoes, and then washed with Fels-Naptha soap, which was customarily used mainly for washing floors. He was thoroughly rinsed, and then the process was repeated until the aunts were satisfied that no trace of skunk smell remained on him. All this time, he bawled loudly and tried to escape their libations.

As things finally calmed somewhat and Donald was brought, still bawling, into the house, they all turned to me for an explanation. I told them the story about the skunk killing and, of course, the whole thing fell on me. I was supposed to look out for my younger brother no matter what, making the entire incident my fault. So Donald acquired a new nickname that lasted his lifetime, and I was awarded the privilege of burying the dead skunk. The name Donald was bestowed with was "Skunker" and even when we had long passed into adulthood, I still heard him addressed as such.

Being younger than me, Donald tended to be coddled by my mother and aunts and, at times, to my mind at least, was treated a bit like royalty. It was with an envious heart that I regarded him and my cousin Billy as I did the chores unfettered by any competition from them. My cousin Barbara I did not hold in the same regard as she, after all, was a girl. Many a cold winter night as I worked on a woodpile, my mind was on my brother and cousin as they sat in warm splendor listening to the radio or playing games by the wood stove in the kitchen. In retrospect, I see that I was the fortunate one. I guess that these things toughened me or perhaps just gave me the exercise my body needed. I grew bigger and stronger in many ways and am now grateful for the favor.

Donald and I grew up with many differences, not the least of which was our physical makeup. While I grew tall, he remained short. My complexion and hair color were dark, his was pale and blond. He was prone to all the childhood diseases that laid him low and I, although I contracted as many as he, shrugged them off with little ill effect.

One particularly hot, dry summer, all of us kids stayed cool by using an old wash bucket filled by hose with water. We stayed in the bright sunlight, jumping in and out of the tub to refresh ourselves. After several hours of exposure, Billy and Donald and Barbara were getting too pink, and after one of the adults noticed their condition, they were hauled into the house out of the sun. I played perhaps another hour by myself, then tired of the game alone and went into the house. I had a slight reddish hue to my skin but did not burn as they did. My dark complexion always tanned to the point where I looked brown throughout the summer and fall months.

By late afternoon, Billy and Barbara were beet red and suffering severe pain at the slightest contact. Donald was face down on his bed, moaning in agony, sick to his stomach, and at times delirious. The doctor had been sent for, and as we awaited his arrival, huge blisters appeared on Donald's back. We were shooed downstairs while the doctor examined him.

After the doctor left, we were told that Donald had heat prostration and that we were not to enter his room, as he needed to rest. After about a week of round-the-clock nursing, we were allowed to stand in the doorway to speak to him briefly. It seemed to me that he spent nearly the rest of the summer there, but of course it was hard to tell because Donald, from that time on, never went out when it was extremely hot, and never again took his shirt off in my memory when he did come out to play.

Billy and Barbara Ewen, my cousins by way of my mother's brother William Ewen, had been left for my grandmother to raise before we joined them. Their father and mother had divorced prior to my mother's divorce. Their mother was more or less a mystery to me as she very seldom had contact with Billy or Barbara, with only the occasional visit, perhaps on their respective birthdays and just prior to Christmas. She would show up, stay long enough to hold a short conversation with my grandmother, leave gifts, talk briefly with Billy and Barbara, and depart. My Uncle William, who lived in a tenement on Barre Street, showed up perhaps a little more often, although in my memory he paid as little attention to their upbringing as possible.

Barbara was dark haired and tall for her age with a good disposition and sense of humor. Billy, on the other hand, was short, with light hair and complexion, and an antagonistic personality. He tried me early in our acquaintance, found himself wanting, and contented himself with putting me down whenever the occasion arose, always at a safe distance. He would make some snide remark only when protection was around in the form of either my grandmother or aunts, then run by them, so by the time I would start for him, they would intervene and prevent his certain demise. Because I had a quick temper but short rage, he would escape until the next incident. He never pulled this sort of thing when within reach or outside the house, as he knew I could catch him.

Like all Celts, I always felt a strong clannish loyalty to family. Brash Billy placed himself in jeopardy with his smart mouth whenever he tried to play on this while away from immediate family. He would provoke a fight with someone and, when they accepted the challenge, he would call for me to defend him. Many times in our early childhood I stepped forward to fight his battles, until the antagonists he provoked learned to ignore him and instead tried to get at him when I wasn't around. This went on for some time, until one day when I decided that his enemy was in the right and declined to fight for him. The beating he took that day almost made up for the bumps and bruises I had incurred as his champion.

20

During the latter years of the 30's, the closest grocery stores below us on Barre Street were Bernasconi's Market, which we rarely entered, Cueto's Market, and Fernandez Market. Cueto's Market was a small hole-in-the-wall-type meat store where Mr. Cueto sold mostly beef that he raised on land elsewhere. Fernandez was slightly more sophisticated, in that it had more store area and therefore more canned goods and products such as laundry items, brooms and assorted packaged items.

When Mr. Charles Fernandez, the proprietor, butchered pigs to sell in his market, he also rendered lard from the fat of the pigs, which was done by heating the fat and skin of the hogs in a large cast iron kettle placed over a fire to melt the fat into lard. After rendering, the pieces of skin left over were cut into short strips and allowed to cool on racks. These pieces, usually curled from the heat and lightly salted, were called scraps. You could buy a small bagful for a nickel, which gave you many days of succulent chewing. We had no cash, but would beg him until he gave us one or two pieces and be merrily on our way chewing our scraps.

He kept a barrel of chlorine bleach in the store. We would be sent with a gallon jug and a nickel to fill it up whenever it was needed at home. He also had a molasses barrel with a spigot used to fill any sized container, and as I remember it was ten cents a quart. Hamburg was a quarter a pound in those days, and cube steak about thirty-five cents a pound. Ice cream cones and chocolate bars were a nickel apiece, a loaf of bread ten cents, and a pound of middlings (uncured bacon) was ten cents. It sounds really good when compared to today's prices, but remember, $15.00 a week was a good salary in those days, and for us kids to find a nickel for such luxuries as ice cream or candy bars was just about impossible.

All of our poultry came live in wooden crates that you paid a deposit on, to be refunded on return to the dealer. Although I don't know the price of a chicken, I do know we worked for our meal. First, we had to kill the bird, then de-feather it, cut it open and pull the guts, hold it over a gas stove to singe the hairy feathers left from plucking, and wash the whole bird thoroughly. It was a dirty, unpleasant job.

Even going to the store in the first place was a problem. If we were lucky, we accompanied an adult and were used only as a beast of burden to carry purchases home. We were not, by Depression standards, poor, but most of the kids who lived on Barre Street at that time were. This set up an antagonistic situation. They formed a gang amongst themselves and were not friendly with us on the hill. If an adult called us to go to the market, we always gathered a group of kids to accompany us on our trek. We also learned short cuts between houses, around gardens and small copses of woods to sneak down, make our purchase, and hie back before being discovered on alien territory. We considered any trip that we were at least not pushed around to be a triumph indeed. A few times, we had to literally fight our way through when their gang was aroused. All this changed as time went by. We all grew older and became familiar with each other by exposure in school and sports, but for a time, it was a fearful event to be asked to go to the store.

21

The fourth of July was a big event, beginning with a parade. Red, white, and blue buntings would be draped from windows of all the downtown buildings. Men wore their summer straw hats, and the ladies with their baby carriages lined the streets, interspersed with roving bands of children. Since this was also the circus season in Vermont, and being the capital of the state, often the circus would parade with other groups and military units.

Overweight World War I veterans dressed in bulging old army uniforms would march. Civil and Spanish American War vets would parade or be driven on floats made expressly for that purpose, and were usually seated behind a woman done up to look like the Statue of Liberty. Speeches by vets or politicians would be given at a grandstand set up in front of City Hall. Afternoons would be devoted, weather permitting, to croquet on the lawns or *tête-à-têtes* on porches spiced with libations of either lemonade or some type of alcohol, while we kids fired off firecrackers in the streets.

One favorite way of using firecrackers was to light a one-incher, cover it quickly with an opened can, and see how high the resulting trapped explosion would send the can. Strips of Ladyfingers (small fire crackers) crackled, interspersed with the loud roar of cherry bombs and larger firecrackers. We also used to go to Sabin's Pasture and, using the larger firecrackers, stick them into cow plops—the fresher the better—to explode them in all directions, the object being to sneak up behind someone otherwise occupied and explode one so as to cover said victim with fresh cow manure.

Fireworks were sold openly in booths set up on Barre Street days before the holiday. By planning ahead, we could pick up a good amount for the event at a minimal cost. As I recall, even cherry bombs, which sounded like cannon fire, sold for three to five cents each, and packages of one inchers sold for five to ten cents for a dozen in each pack. Sparklers sold for about a penny apiece. Larger rockets and Roman candles were out of our price range, and were usually handled by adults anyway.

These would be brought out of almost every household in the evening to be lit or fired on side or back lawns. Banging sounds would be heard amidst whooshing and the sharp crack of small fireworks, along with shrieks of delight, as the neighborhood came alive. We kids would wave our sparklers and dance around with total abandon, enjoying not only the show but the fact that we were allowed to stay up much later than usual this one night. When the fireworks had been exhausted, everyone would retire to their porches in the warm summer night air, and low conversation could be heard, punctuated by bursts of laughter. This was one of the few times we children kept quiet and listened to the adults, hoping they wouldn't notice us among them and send us to bed. It usually worked for quite a spell until, during a lull in their conversation, someone would say those dreaded words, "Off to bed!" and another glorious Fourth would be ended.

22

Milk in those days was either whole or pasteurized, whole being as it came from the cow in all its goodness, loaded with butterfat and occasionally with undulant fever. If you knew your source—that is to say, personally knew the farmer who produced the milk—you might prefer the whole milk. However, as most people didn't, or you had milk delivery like we did, it came bottled and pasteurized in quart bottles.

The bottles were made of clear glass, with a bulging top of about two and a half to three inches high that formed a chamber of sorts for the cream to rise into. The dairy provided a peculiar shaped spoon that bent decidedly so you could open the bottle, insert the spoon to trap the cream in the top, and pour it off without mixing it with the milk. Some people would go directly to the dairy to have small aluminum cans filled there. These had tops that pushed on, each container holding about a half gallon of milk. They paid less for their milk, naturally, as it saved bottling and delivery charges. You could also buy cream separately in half-pint bottles.

All the cream in the quart bottles was not removed with the cream spoon maneuver, so if you got the bottle of milk first and poured carefully onto your morning oatmeal, you could get a good-sized portion of cream as well. Naturally, this became a bone of contention among the family, and we started many days with the unpleasantness of argument.

We may have had little in the way of material things and certainly had few luxuries, but we did eat well. Brownies and cookies of several varieties were always on hand, baked mostly by Aunt Edith, but occasionally by another of my aunts. These were doled out to us kids one at a time as dessert at mealtimes. They were kept on a broad shelf above the cellar stairs in covered tins. Of course, one at mealtime hardly sated our desire, and we schemed how to circumvent the tight and squeaky door that barred us from our epicurean longings.

Knowing better than to enter through the kitchen door, I figured that I might be able to accomplish my mission by attacking from the cellar. There were two ways I could enter the cellar, not counting the cellar door in the kitchen. One was through the outside door to the storage room under the kitchen, which was usually bolted shut. If I could unbolt it while removing the furnace ashes for outside disposal and somehow leave it unbolted, I'd have a clear shot. However, when I tried this, it did not work, as the outside door was somewhat warped and wouldn't stay shut without being bolted.

My second chance was through two small cellar windows along the outside foundation. One was used to load wood into the cellar, and the other hadn't been opened in years. It was directly beside the furnace, and to throw wood there would have caused damage. I managed to work on opening this window whenever I had an errand that sent me to the cellar, and finally freed it enough so that, if I could open it from the outside, slip through and shut it behind me unnoticed, I would be in position to strike. I finally built my courage up and did make it inside, only to discover that now I had another problem. The cellar was pitch black without lights, which were controlled by a switch at the top of the stairs. I waited in the dark for my eyes to adjust to the faint light from those two small windows, crept slowly up the creaky stairs, and carefully lifted the top. After grabbing two brownies, I cautiously replaced the cover and crept back down. My scheme had worked and I exited the cellar by reverse procedure.

I worked this scheme several times, until one day as I crept across the cellar floor, the kitchen door opened and the lights went on. There I was, exposed. I dashed behind the furnace as feet and legs appeared, coming down the stairs. Crouched down behind the furnace where the light scarcely penetrated, I watched Aunt Edith go by into the storage room, from which she soon returned with a few jars of canned goods. She never saw me but proceeded back upstairs, shut off the lights and closed the door to the kitchen. I shook in terror for some time and then made my retreat. This close call ended my forays to the cellar. I knew the consequences of my being caught were greater than my desire for sweets. I never attempted the journey again.

The rule in our household was that if you ate your meal you were entitled to dessert. If you did not eat your meal completely, then no dessert. It was about this time that the culinary tastes of my aunts took a decidedly bizarre turn for the worse. Such delicacies as pickled tripe, fried squid, chicken livers, Rocky Mountain oysters, and calf brains began to be included in our regular diet. These did not appeal to a child in the slightest, at least not to me. While the others struggled to eat some of these with the express purpose of not being denied dessert, my Celtic stubbornness asserted itself and I refused. Even the dangled carrot of cookies, pie, cake or other pastry failed to make me eat that type of meal. On those nights, I was allowed cereal instead of the meal, but no dessert. This went on for quite a while, and by the time we returned to what I call normal meals; I no longer cared greatly for desserts. This caused some consternation, I am sure, for as I lost interest in sweets, the adults lost control over me.

23

The radio was situated in our formal living room with its pocket doors that would be opened on Sunday nights for family entertainment. We kids were not to touch this altar of the airwaves but were to sit quietly and just listen. The strains of dramatic music, mingling with the deep tones of the radio actors, were a source of excitement and tension as the plots enthralled us all.

The sounds of *Sergeant Preston of the Yukon*, *Jack Armstrong the All American Boy*, the enigmatic *Shadow* and *Green Hornet* reverberated in the room, describing dramatic pictures you could almost feel as well as hear. The voices of Walter Winchell and John Caltonburne commanded our every attention to their deep modulated tones. No one would miss a word of his or her discourse on the news or commentary, which I followed with anxious trepidation.

Then the lighter side of the evening would begin with *Fibber Magee and Molly* and their assorted comic characters, followed by *The Phil Harris Show*, then on to the main attraction of the evening, *The Jack Benny Show*. This was the highlight of the evening with all of its characters—Mary, Rochester, and Dennis, who not only played comedy in a high squeaky voice, but also sang in a beautiful tenor the popular songs of the day. Combined with the self-deprecatory comedy of Jack himself, this was awaited all week long.

The only other time we were allowed to listen to the radio was on fight nights, particularly the championship fights of Joe Louis, which round to round excited much comment from the adults. Joe Louis had the habit of winning his fights in the early rounds, usually by clear knockouts. The build-ups for his clashes went on for months, even the weigh-ins were cause for intense interest. Max Baer, Tony Gallento, Max Schmelling, and Primo Canara were the main challengers of the time, all of which were dispatched by the Mighty Joe.

During promotion for his upcoming challenge for the heavyweight championship, Primo Canara, known as *The Italian Giant*, visited a close relative on Barre Street named Ribelli, whose daughter I knew from school. I was invited to meet him at the Ribelli home, which I did with great anticipation.

He was a huge man of perhaps six feet six or seven, with massive shoulders and a huge hand that seemed to me the size of a baseball glove. He spoke only Italian, but seemed to enjoy the adoration of all the children who were invited to meet him. He shook all our hands very gently, commenting in Italian, and smiling a wide smile as he kneeled down to get closer to our size. I was very impressed, and very pleased and excited to actually have personal contact with him. He proved to have an Achilles heel in the form of a glass jaw when Joe Louis summarily KO'd him in an early round, but he still symbolizes for me raw human power tempered by mild manner and gentle action.

24

In the early fall of each year, boxcar upon boxcar would arrive behind the Bernasconi Market. These would be filled with stacked wooden crates of bursting Concord grapes flowing with purple juices. The Italians, Spaniards, and Slavs from all over the area would gather to collect what I suppose was their portion of the shipment, and in a few days all the cars would be empty. It was now *grappa*, or grape season. The fruit would be turned into several liquid refreshments according to the tastes of each ethnic group.

The Italians and Spaniards would first press the grapes and store them for wine. Then the less-fresh grapes were pressed, reserving the liquid to make a strong brandy known as *grappa*. The alcohol content of the distillate that ran through the myriad coils of their homemade stills rose in proof until it hit almost absolute. Potency would vary as well as clarity, going from light amber to clear as spring water. Great pride was taken in producing the clearest, most potent product. The individuals involved in the production of grappa swelled with this pride when they referred to their liquor, and would eagerly show each visitor by holding a clean glass up to the light to exhibit the clarity of this ambrosia of the grape.

Since this occurred only a short time since the repeal of prohibition, it amazed us that law enforcement allowed this. However, we learned that you were allowed to make wine and this liquor in certain quantities for your own use. There was the rub. Who knew, without inspection of each premise, how much each individual produced? Also, they were not averse to selling the grappa in quarts and pints of canning jars.

The solution to this mystery was solved when sheriffs, uniformed police, and others would show up at certain homes, stay inside for perhaps an hour, and return carrying plain paper bags which they gingerly placed on the seats of their automobiles before driving off. They would show up at regular intervals which we were sure were payoffs, giving the makers license to peddle the product.

Several families would show the effects of this enterprise in the form of new objects overtly displayed. Cars, boats, and clothing appeared in good years of the grape in families where the only apparent source of income was the granite sheds. Several widows managed to raise families through grappa sales. Every home had the acrid-sweet smell of old wooden casks saturated by grape juice that permeated the whole house, which was particularly strong in grape season.

25

Along with the process of canning fruits and vegetables, the bottling of root beer was also a tradition in our household. When others in our neighborhood bottled their wine and grappa, we were engaged in preparing a supply of a somewhat dubious libation known as root beer, a soda of questionable contents, as from year to year, the adults in our family supposedly learned new techniques in search of perfection. The science of root beer making could be compared to astrology in its exactness.

Out would come the copper canner that we bathed in as youngsters. This was filled with water and set to boil on the gas stove. The root beer extract, along with measured amounts of sugar, would be stirred in carefully and allowed to cool slightly. The prewashed bottles would be lined up, and small amounts of yeast would be spooned carefully into them just prior to being filled with the cooling mixture from the copper canner. We had a single bottle capper, and each bottle, when filled to a prescribed level, was capped carefully and firmly in the capper. The capper was a cast iron instrument with a long handle that was raised to accept the bottle. The cap was carefully placed on top of the bottle, and the handle compressed, forcing the cap onto the bottle top and gripping its sides to secure it.

Once the bottles were filled, they were taken down to the back cellar and placed on the shelves for storage and aging. Usually the cellar remained quite cool, but it had one drawback. A shade over the lone window helped to cut the heat of the afternoon sun, which glared on the back of our house in the afternoon. There being but one light in that room, operated by a pull string which frequently broke upon being pulled to trip the switch, the only recourse to achieve light was to raise the shade so that the room would be lit by sunlight. This worked well, as long as whoever raised the shade also lowered it when they went back upstairs.

Many times the shade was forgotten in the haste of gathering vegetables and fruit from the canning section for a meal being prepared at that moment. Consequently, the sun often shown on those bottles of root beer for days at a time, and the heat magnifying through the glass of the bottle raised the temperature of the contents, as the fermenting yeast solution became an expansive gas with no vent.

That's when the pows of explosive gas burst the caps on the bottles and spewed the liquid all over the room underneath. I could safely say that out of one hundred bottles, perhaps thirty to forty might survive the onslaught. Blame for the exploding elixir would be placed upon the originator of the latest innovation in formula. This would be lavishly pointed out to that person for weeks on end. I knew that it mattered little what formula was used. What really mattered to me was the fact that I would be the one to clean it up.

We also made our own ice cream. Ice cream was a rare treat for our taste buds as children, the adults being the only ones with access to store-bought varieties. We could get a taste, however, when homemade ice cream was made.

We had a bucket-type maker that was hand-cranked. For the price of cranking and keeping ice and salt around the freezing chamber, we were allowed a small amount of the finished product. The chamber held about a quart of ice cream that was emptied upon freezing, and was promptly refilled with more mixture. It took a lot of ice cream to feed the group that gathered for Sunday dinner.

I remember grinding away for what seemed like most of a Saturday morning, only to be rewarded with a bowl so small as to be eclipsed by a five-cent cone. Our hands froze from handling and breaking ice into small pieces to fit between the barrel outside and the chamber that turned by the crank inside. It had to be carefully loaded or we couldn't turn it, yet full enough to cool the cream in the chamber. The rock salt also had to be broken so as to fit with the ice. It was only used in specific quantities, as too much would melt the ice too quickly. It was an exacting job.

What looked at first like fun soon paled to drudgery as we ground and filled and broke ice and salt. Our hands would shrivel and pucker and blister before we finished the job. Somehow, as we sat trying to make our reward last, it all seemed worth it, and we savored every morsel and licked the bowl.

26

One of the things that my contemporaries and I did was collect things. Anything that did not cost money was fair game. Rocks, shells, bottle caps, bottles, matchbooks—an endless list—were sought avidly. Marbles, or allies as we called them, were one of this group that for a time became the main interest of us all. The usual games we played with them involved seeing how close to a wall you could flick or throw your marble from a previously agreed line. For another, we dug a small hole in the earth and, in a determined circle around it, tried to flick a marble into the hole. The closest marble took all the marbles used.

But the most profitable way to collect marbles was to find a cigar box with a lid that flipped up, and make a small hole that an alley or marble would just barely pass through in the middle of the lid. The shooter stood above the box placed on the ground with feet spread at either end of the box and dropped the marble through the hole. Odds were given, depending on the hole size. For instance, if a marble just barely fit and needed a slight tap to go through, odds of up to 3-5 to 1 were given, meaning the shooter collected up to five marbles if he made the drop. Any misses became the property of the box holder. If you practiced enough, you could get pretty good at hitting the hole just right and collect quite a few marbles. Of course, the odds were with the box holder and he could collect a lot of marbles before making a payoff. Almost every boy had his marble box, which he carried to school every day. Mahlon Garback was the best shooter and also carried the tightest box. He collected seven or eight gallon glass jugs full of allies before the craze died.

Bottle caps were another collection craze at that time. There were no easy-open twist caps then and you needed an opener to get the cap off. If you did it right, the cap flipped off in good condition, but if you didn't take care, you bent the cap as you used the opener. Only those caps in good condition were collectable, and those with any damage were not acceptable and were discarded.

Pabst, Peels, and Ballantynes were common. Sometimes the capping machine had double- or triple-capped the bottles. This molded the two or three caps firmly together and increased their value to us. Rarer caps from brands not familiar to our area were more valuable. We rated the caps for trade purposes. For instance, one Peels Creme Ale was worth at least three of more common caps.

I'm sure we all drove the adults to distraction with our hoards of marbles, bottle caps, and other collections in bags, jars, or boxes stashed around our rooms. Some of us collected stamps as well, and I was one of them. By the time I had lost interest in stamp collecting, I had filled several books.

All of these collections, including my rose quartz of many hues, old automobile lights, and other items were summarily disposed of by my mother while I was in the service. Some of these things would by now have been worth a fair amount, and I have always regretted that I was not able to hold onto them until they increased in value.

27

In 1938, the CCC built, among many other projects, the Montpelier swimming pool on upper Elm Street. Up until that time, the only places to swim in the area were two river holes; one in the Dog River known as Devil's Ledge, the other on the north branch of the Winooski River known as the Ice House.

The Ice House was a pool formed by a short dam made for ice cutting operations during wintertime. The Ice House itself was a high building that flanked one side of the pool. Drownings had occurred in both places and diving into ledges or boulders had resulted in severe injuries. You swam at your own risk with no lifeguards or supervision and, of course, we were not allowed in either area.

Up until the building of the municipal pool, the only place we could sneak off to was the brook that bisected Sabin's Pasture. Mr. Babic, known by his first name Drago, had made a pool by damming a small stream where he would bathe daily in the summer months. He was a blacksmith in one of the stone sheds. His job was to remake broken tools and to reshape wedges that had been distorted while splitting the huge slabs of granite.

Every evening at about five o'clock he would walk bare-chested with a towel over his shoulder up from Charles Street where he lived and head for Sabin's pasture to partake of his daily ablutions. We used his pool as a swimming hole on hot days, standing in a depth over our waists. The pool covered an area of perhaps ten feet by eight feet and did not give us much swimming room, but was sufficiently big enough that we learned to dogpaddle and float.

With the advent of the municipal pool opening, we all paraded up over Seminary Hill, down East State Street, up Main Street to the Spring Street Bridge, then over to Elm to get to the pool. It was a long, hot walk to get way up Elm Street to the Recreation Field. After swimming for an afternoon, we had the long, hot walk back home to contend with, often arriving there as hot as when we left and exhausted as well.

I had been learning to dive, and on one of my leaps from the high board, I had gone into the water at a high angle. On my pullout at the bottom of the pool, I had scraped the little toe on my right foot on the asphalt surface. It was a small abrasion and I didn't give it a second thought. After swimming, I replaced my soiled socks and ratty sneakers and walked the two miles home. I was so tired when I arrived home, I didn't even put a Band-Aid over the cut. It hurt a little when I walked on my right foot for a few days, and on examination it showed signs of infection. There were no antibiotics at that time; even penicillin was not discovered until World War II. The only methods of treatment were decidedly crude. Infections were referred to as blood poisoning, which was the diagnosis given me. I had to soak my foot in hot water laced with Epsom salts and then cover the area with Icthamol Ointment, a tar preparation meant to draw the infection out. The treatment did not work. Inflammation flared up my leg. It swelled my groin area with a great bulge, hard as a rock, where the lymphatic glands trapped the infection.

The surgery to lance the infection was my first experience in a hospital. A wick, or drain was put in my groin to allow drainage of the gland, and Lysol soaks of my foot continued until my own defenses repelled the infection. It took a recovery period of two weeks before I was allowed out of bed and on to the porch at home for a restricted week of continuous supervision. After more than a month of treatment, I was pronounced cured and allowed back to normal life. I guess I was lucky, as two other people in town died that summer of blood poisoning.

My next bout with hospitalization came the following summer with appendicitis. Rushed to the hospital for emergency surgery, my appendix was removed through a large incision made in my abdomen. Another drain was left for weeks before being removed, along with the stitches used to suture the surgical wound. The scar left from this operation is still sensitive to the touch and even bed covers brushing against it sets me off.

The only other real injury I sustained in my childhood came as a result of playing baseball. I had never had the arm to play most positions on a baseball diamond. My throws from any of the outfield positions were woefully inadequate and usually ended up dribbling on the ground far short of their intended target. Flights of birds or the movement of clouds also easily distracted me. Fascination with insects amongst the grass at my feet was apt to slow my reflexes to a speed much slower than required of a base position. The only two options left open to me were catcher or pitcher, as these required my constant attention.

Having played catcher for some time adequately, I longed for a change and opted for a pitching position. Trying out the new position, I found the short distance from the mound to the catcher's box to be just right for my dubious talents. I soon developed an adequate fastball and a very good curve, supplemented by a change-of-pace knuckle ball that dropped unerringly just before passing over the plate. Puffed up by the surprisingly efficient manner with which I executed the position of pitcher, I confidently (for a while) rejoiced in the satisfaction of power over the batters. I had gotten to where I could retire the other side in rapid one, two, three succession and was being accorded the acclaim due my prowess.

One day, with the sun beating down on the field, I faced a batter I had struck out many times in the past. I hurled two fastballs across the plate with which he came nowhere near to connecting. Confident, I hurled my last strike at him. Before I could straighten up from my follow-through, the crack of the bat and the shock of the ball striking me right in the eye came at the same time.

I had thrown what was called a Texas leaguer, which meant the ball, when struck, did not follow an upward trajectory, but came more or less flat straight for the pitcher's mound. Sometimes it becomes an easy out as the pitcher catches it on its return, or ducks to let the shortstop or second baseman handle it. This time it happened too fast for me to react. Consequently, all I heard was the bat crack before I was aware of stars in my vision. Then I blanked out.

I came to in a swelter of pain with a cluster of kids all around. My left eye throbbed, and even the light allowed by my closed eyelids was glaring, exacerbating the agony. My nose, which I was sure was broken, also radiated extreme pain and seemed to swell as I lay there. In a teary, half-blind state, I was helped home, where cold packs and the eventual promise of ice cream gradually reduced the pain to bearable.

The next couple of weeks were without doubt the worst I ever knew. Having to wear a patch over the swollen, blind eye, which, if I forced it open, returned my efforts with a horrible blurred yet blazing light, was pure hell. The instant agony and fear of permanent blindness gnawed at my mind. However, being a child, I finally healed physically. But never again could I challenge a batter from the pitcher's mound. Instead, I regularly banished myself to right field where the least number of balls were hit, and happily returned to bird, cloud, and insect watching with contentment. My aspirations of a professional career in baseball had died in one agonizing moment.

Other sports kept us busy. Mr. Frail, who lived in a house on the corner of Sabin and College Streets, had a large barn-like garage whose second floor had a high ceiling with a basket at one end. He rented it out at the rate of ten cents an hour to cover the cost of the lights. Jim Seivwright would pay the light costs and we would play half court basketball games. I never grasped the idea of no contact, so I usually fouled out at almost the inception of the game. I also could not seem to grasp the art of dribbling, since I couldn't concentrate on but one thing at a time. Nor did I have the interest, because basketball season came at the best part of hunting season. In short, I was a lousy basketball player with no talent. With my lack of talent, I didn't become involved in playing basketball until sometime in high school where, even then, I was no shining star.

Football, on the other hand, I thoroughly enjoyed. I loved the contact and roughness of the sport and, because of my running ability, could go at it with the best of them. This also vied with hunting season, and I agonized between the two all my young life. All that was required for football was a field to play on and players to play with, the number of the latter being however many showed up. Even with the game in progress, new arrivals were inserted into some position as they came. The thrill of tucking the ball under an arm and smashing into a hoard of would-be tacklers, or tackling hard enough to stop someone in their tracks was very satisfying indeed. Since most injuries occurred by being hit, being the hitter, which I enjoyed, seemed to keep me from injury. Football became my prime sport in its season, surpassing all others.

The Italians, who lived mainly on Barre Street when I was growing up, had a game they played that was much like bowling, only it was played on a court with boarded sides on level, packed earth. One court in particular enclosed the whole back area of the Ribelli land, and even had lights strung across its center for night use. We kids did not understand the game, but watched anyway, waiting for roars of "Bocce!" There was much imbibing of the homemade wine, and merry, joyful laughter accompanying the progress of the matches where all involved seemed to enjoy themselves. Now we play the same game on our lawns with much gusto and enjoyment, having learned the rules ourselves, and we now know that what we had thought was petty bickering was actually measuring space between the balls, an important part of the game. We, of course, never bicker.

There were several tennis courts on Seminary Hill besides the one at the college. The largest and best kept belonged to the Parkers, whose house was on the corner of Sabin and College Streets. They had a large formal garden, which sided on College Street. Beyond this, on a large terrace some feet down from the garden, was a double court. This was surrounded by a ten-foot fence with a gated locked. The Parkers consisted of Mr. and Mrs. Parker and their children, Harry, the oldest, and Charlie. On summer evenings, they would play matches with friends on the courts, then return through the garden to a slate patio with wicker furniture, and tables set for a festive evening meal. To us, it was a display of a more genteel life. We were awed, particularly by their mode of dress—white tennis shorts and shirts with white tennis sweaters for when the evening cooled or the day was cloudy. Charlie seemed to me to be the epitome of coolness and grace, and he became a sort of hero to look up to in my youth. He was always casual and friendly, with an air of self-assurance that could have been envied but was not. I would meet him walking by the college and he would always greet me with a smile, and sometimes hold a short conversation with me. I would be thrilled just to have been spoken to.

One of my greatest hand-me-downs was a white tennis sweater with a V-neck trimmed in maroon and navy blue stripes that Victor outgrew. I wore it proudly until it disintegrated from wear. I never learned nor had the time to play tennis, but the sweater somehow made me feel like the hero of my youth.

28

My aunt Nonie had married my Uncle Victor Lavin, a cattle dealer. This created great changes in our lives. For one thing, it gave me a chance to drive through the rural countryside and learn about the lives of the people who ran the farms. It was a very different life from the small town/city of Montpelier with its provincial sophistication and social caste system.

On weekends, and at different times during the summer months, I would accompany Victor on his rounds from farm to farm, in the course of which we entered many barns and pastures, accompanied by farmers. You could tell the successful farmers from the others by the way the barns were kept. Some farms were decidedly marginal, with uncleaned gutters and heavy scent, bedding so sparse as to be nothing but muck, and cattle caked with urine and dung. The successful farms were clean and airy with deep beds of shavings and clean gutters, doors that opened and shut easily, and whitewashed walls. We made our way to both kinds, buying decent cattle at some, canners (those cattle so poor they were butchered only for dog food), and bobs, which were bull calves used for the same reason.

At the end of a tour, we would unload at Vic's father's barn located on Main Street in Barre where the Elks Club is now situated. We would put the cattle in the barn, feed them, feed the calves, and be done for that day. When a suitable load had been collected over a period of two weeks or more, Victor would load up the truck with the cattle and bobs and drive to Manchester, New Hampshire to a large slaughterhouse, sell his load and return home. In the summer months or during school vacations, I would sometimes accompany him. It was a long trip with my motion sickness to contend with, but I couldn't turn down the opportunity to see the scenery and the cities we passed through. I suffered through most of every trip, but still enjoyed them.

On one of our winter jaunts through Moretown, Waitsfield and Warren on a cold blustery day with the thermometer hovering well below the zero mark, we stopped for lunch at the Warren Store. Purchasing a loaf of bread, some mustard, assorted cold cuts, and a generous slice of sharp store cheese, we returned to the truck and made sandwiches. It was my first introduction to hearty Vermont cheddar cheese, and after eating my sandwich; I definitely found it to my liking. I nibbled on this magnificent cheese as we stopped at farms and while I waited in the truck when Victor went to the farmhouses to ask if they had cows or calves for sale. Due to the severe weather, Victor couldn't shut the truck off and leave it for however long it took to negotiate deals, because in that amount of time the windshield would thickly frost to the point that it would have to be scraped and the truck motor warmed back up again. So I sat in relative comfort, heater blasting, munching on cheese.

As we passed from Warren Common down into Moretown Common, I started to expel gas in rich pungent odors. Victor, of course, reacted with loud oaths as he swiftly rolled his side window down, allowing blasts of cold air into the truck cab. This meant he had to close the window with more curses before he froze. We continued on in this manner, with much cursing and many blasts of cold air, until we reached Barre. Victor had by that time purchased a farm at the top of Trow Hill and a house adjacent to it. As we were climbing Trow Hill, the old Dodge truck in low gear due to the incline we were on, I glanced at Victor's face, lighted by the dim light of the truck's instrument panel, and ascertained him to be straining in some way.

Suddenly, a surprised look came over his face and he tromped on the gas pedal. The truck leaped forward, roaring up the hill. Without a word to me, we reached the top of the hill, sped by the barn, turned down the crossroads and roared into the driveway of the house. As the truck slowed down, he leapt from the cab and raced for the house. I shoved over and managed to stop the truck before it crashed into the garage. He had thought he would expel a little gas, too, and was straining to pay me back for the day, only to soil his shorts woefully, hence the race for home. I have never forgotten his actions to this day and neither have I let him forget.

Another occasion involved a first time calf heifer that had been kept in a large pasture at the north end of Barre, owned by Victor's father. She calved sooner than expected and kept her calf hidden in the dense brush-clogged gullies that lined a steep section of the pasture. We tried to find the calf so that we could use it to coax her out in the open where we thought we could control her. Instead, she turned into a raging beast that charged anyone getting close to these ravines. This was at a time before de-horning had become popular as a means of preventing serious damage by an animal. She had wicked horns that came to a sharp point and no one wanted to challenge her.

Finally, Victor decided enough was enough. Obtaining a two by four about five to six feet long, he planned to put an end to this fiasco. As he approached the area, the heifer charged him. He swung his weapon and knocked her right horn almost off her head. It dangled by a strip of skin as she turned to charge him again, no doubt enraged by pain as well as maternal instinct. Victor decided that retreat was better than valor, threw the two by four at her and ran as if his life depended on it for the fence. He barely made it over the fence, snagging his pants so that they tore a wide rent before she arrived and hit the fence behind him. The fence held, and she drew back to bellow at him, all the time shaking her head in fury, with that broken horn flopping against her head. After several more attempts to rope her in western fashion, resulting only in comic gyrations to escape her charges, she was summarily shot by my irate uncle, who by this time was so enraged that thoughts of profit were definitely outweighed by aggravation.

All in all, I learned a lot about animal husbandry and farming by haying, milking, mucking out gutters, feeding calves, and doing general chores about Victor's barn as I grew up, certainly enough to know it was not for me. And all for the salary of wind.

29

As World War II approached, so did rationing, particularly gas rationing. Traffic slowed to a snail's pace. Unless you were engaged in what was considered an essential industry, you were reduced to paltry proportions of gas to run your car. The few cars in our neighborhood fell under the lowest priority for gas, and therefore were little used until a viable block market was established. Victor, being in the cattle business, was considered an agricultural adjunct and therefore had high priority on the rationing scale.

On some Saturday afternoons, Vic would bring the large cattle truck to Montpelier and park it in front of our house. It was my job to muck out the truck, and then sweep all around the body, chipping off caked manure on its insides. Then I would hose the entire inside and scrub it with stiff brushes until all was clean, wash the entire outside off, and allow the whole thing to dry inside and out. The next morning, I would spread two or three fresh bales of hay in the truck body and place assorted chairs on the blanket of hay.

Kate Colombo would arrive, and the families in the neighborhood would come with baskets of prepared food, which was carefully loaded among the chairs. Everyone would pile in to fill the chairs, with the kids sitting on the hay. Away we would go, enclosed in the darkened cattle truck, whose only light showed through at the top of the tailgate from a strip about three inches to the roof of the body. Kate Colombo kept us singing the old songs, such as *Moonlight Bay*, *Old Mill Stream*, *Loch Lomond*, *The Old Gray Mare*, and *The Bear and the Mountain*, sung with gusto by all.

We would sway and bump, bracing ourselves as best we could, sometimes rocking off the truck body walls and trying to roll with the bumps that we couldn't see, especially on unanticipated corners. We always made our destination without serious injury and in good humor. We would usually end up at Groton Forest or Bear Mountain State Park and embark from our dubious ark in anticipation of the day. The adults would garner their goody baskets and secure occupancy of the picnic tables provided. While they were busy, we kids would race all over the place exploring the area, climbing the fire tower or just playing. After fires had been built in the fireplaces provided, and hamburgers, hot dogs, or chicken had been cooked over the grates, we would be called to the picnic lunch.

All manner of food would be spread on the picnic tables, and we got to choose what we wanted to eat. After the meal, we would have to help with the cleanup before being released to play again. Sometimes baseball games would be organized, which included some of the adults, and we would spend a pleasant afternoon together.

As the day lengthened and the sun began to fade, we would reluctantly pack the truck and leave for home. The singing would again commence, continuing until, one by one, we kids fell asleep, lulled by the motions of the truck and fatigue. Upon arrival home, we would help unload the truck, put things away, and stagger to our respective beds, totally exhausted but warmed by the pleasant memories of the day.

30

Life in the 1930's, although hard at times, was not without its better points. We children did not feel deprived as we all shared what small luxury there was among us and felt no envy for the good fortunes of others, although there were few.

It was a time when children were instilled with common values. People were inherently honest, sympathetic, helpful and charitable in their daily pursuits. Crime, if there was any, was at a minimum in our rural area. No one locked doors or barns nor felt a need to. Even our vandalism was of the prank variety and not intended to destroy. With the exception of raiding gardens or fruit trees of the well off, we made little disturbance of others. Posting of property against trespass was a rare thing and generally ignored, even by law enforcement. There were a few who would yell at us kids if we crossed their land so we generally avoided it. There again, with one notable exception of the Seminary property, which was ruled by a crabby janitor who considered the grounds his personal domain, everyone's property was respected and their rights and rules adhered to.

Everyone's parents became your personal authority; the cardinal sin of the times was disrespect. An importune or smart remark to any adult brought swift physical punishment on the spot and again on your arrival home. There was little, if any, recrimination between authorities within our society. A child was a child and had no rights and we well knew it. There was no malicious intent in these tenets, only a certainty of rapid punishment for an act not tolerated. Abuse was something horrid, the word used particularly to describe bad treatment of animals or property. Facial or verbal expressions did not qualify as abuse in the way they might today.

Swearing or filthy language was not accepted by the society of the 30's. It did have devotees amongst peer groups, but was not considered acceptable in any other company. If slips were made, instant punishment was enacted—slaps in the face, application of soap to the mouth, and banishment to bed, swiftly administered. Hence, we were very careful with our language and we made every conscious effort not to fail. What is now considered common in those times would have been met with what was called "a trip to the woodshed," which was punishment meted out with the aid of straps, belts, or switches upon the gluteal area of the offender. Transgressions of all sorts were met with these methods and one soon learned to behave.

Adult society was something you joined only with age when you grew into it. Otherwise, children and adults were separate entities not to be mixed except through the discretion of adults at their leisure. Frankly, we liked it that way, as it was only a source of embarrassment for us in those rare times we were included in adult pursuits. We had our own interests and enjoyed each other's company too much to be concerned by the lack of adult participation in our lives.

Honor, integrity, and eagerness to lend a helping hand to any endeavor were highly valued. Dishonor could come from merely not being an active participant in any action discerned to be of import to the community. In other words, one did not stand by and allow bad things to take place. In the case of a bully in a fight, one was expected to come to the aid of the weaker opponent. In the event that someone was in peril, one was expected to rescue that person, regardless of personal danger. I am sure that this philosophy was what maintained the heroics of World War II that followed the thirties in no small degree.

A man's word was his bond and woe unto him who broke it. To lie was a sin so great it was never forgotten, even long decades into the future. His peers stained the liar with the "mark of Cain" forever. The expression "Liar, liar, pants on fire!" was a strong admonition that the perpetrator was on his way to the fires of Hell.

The 30's were an age of testing your mettle, and of acts of mercy, charity, and integrity. Through these attributes, this nation overcame a time of want and need just in the nick of time for the test of total war. We who were its children learned the lessons of thrift through necessity. We learned that honor, family and neighbors were of high importance and of great value.

31

Washington County Grammar School was torn down during the summer between my fifth and sixth grades, and in September we entered the new Union School for the first time. The new school had been in progress for a full year, built on the former campus of the old school. The old Washington County Grammar School had been built on a slight rise of land rather close to the Hubbard Street embankment. Its approach from what is now known as School Street was lined with massive elms that extended from Loomis Street to the imposing structure. To the left of the street was a flat campus that extended the full length of Park Avenue. It was on this area that the new school was built. The right-hand side of the extension of School Street had a very slight rise from the street that was used to present a pageant every spring before school was let out for the summer. This was the highlight of the school year and much effort was expended to ensure an impressive performance.

The old school was an imposing edifice of three stories, with huge windows overlooking the front entrance, behind which a staircase rose from the first floor to a landing at the second floor level, and rose again to the third floor. This presented a dizzying view to us when descending the stairs from the third floor. As you looked straight ahead through the huge windows, which had a short sill, the impression of open space was overwhelming. With my acrophobia, I imagined being tripped or pushed through this window and falling to the ground outside, which was not only two full stories, but also a sharp drop to the street another six to eight feet beyond. It was with much trepidation and fear that I managed to get up and down these stairs. Fortunately, except for assemblies and one play held in the auditorium on the third floor, I didn't have to go up there much before we moved to the new school.

The wood-floored hallways and classrooms with their high ceilings of ten feet or more creaked or thundered as classes began or ended. The open slate-walled basements wafted their odors throughout the school. At the bottom of the concrete stairs taken from the outside door to the basement of the old Washington County Grammar School was a huge room for the boys only. On the right wall were huge panels of slate that encompassed the entire wall, over which a long pipe with holes at intervals allowed a slow, thin cascade of water to flow down the slates, ending in a shallow gutter of about 4" in depth and 8" in width. This in turn flowed to a corner of the cellar where it disappeared down a large drain. This was our urinal. Though designed for constant flow, most times it was impeded by paper and cigarette butts, all of which enhanced the smell of stale urine that permeated the entire room. The end wall was clear of obstruction and the left wall housed about six stalls containing toilets whose purpose was to allow for the inevitable #2 as opposed to #1 of the urinals. The raising of a hand in class with the first finger extended notified the teacher of your need. Permission was given and time for only that purpose was allowed. If two fingers were extended on the raised hand, then more time was allowed.

The stairs to the first floor were behind a door at the top of the concrete steps whose top formed a landing. The only other egress to the room was to the boiler room, manned by the head janitor and kept locked from the inside. These stairs led directly to the hall on the first floor and allowed the odors supposedly confined in the basement to waft up the stairway and creep down the halls. That pungent odor was further enhanced at times by plugged toilets that overflowed into the main basement, and since our head janitor was also our only janitor, it was sometimes hours before it was cleaned up. What the girls' basement looked like I know not, but surmise that, although as archaic as our side, it had to have been much cleaner.

Most discipline was taken care of at the class level. Certain cases were sent to the office where Mr. Clossey, the Principal, exercised his own particular brand of punishment. He would wield his shortened yardstick with punitive sternness while you stood with outstretched hand. The number of cracks on the hand was determined by the severity of the offense or by his temper at the time. Wild stories were told with somewhat inflated pride of the individual punishment suffered and the courage of the one being punished. I never had the opportunity for first-hand experience although I suspect I might have come quite close.

The new school with its solid halls, tiled floors in the classrooms, superb lighting, and ventilation was a new experience for us all. The gymnasium and auditorium were impressive indeed and put to good use by us all. Calisthenics and basketball, as well as a hot lunch program, were experienced for the first time, and plays or other entertainment in the auditorium frequently broke dull school days.

We watched the demise of the old school as it was swiftly brought down. The area where it had stood became a temporary playground of sorts. Thus the transition from old to modern and the progress of education came to us. Although it helped as far as comfort was concerned, I doubt it made much difference in scholarship.

After the old school was removed, the last portion of the new Union School was constructed. Landscaping was completed and the site of the old school was our new playground. The hillside rising to the old primary school on East State Street was also landscaped and new maple trees planted, I assume to help prevent the steep incline from erosion. These were saplings on the order of eight to ten feet tall, with a diameter of two to three inches, and were braced by staked wires to the ground.

One day Frank Fallacci decided it would be great to carve his initials in one of them and proceeded to do so on both sides of the tree. This had the effect of girdling the bark. Someone either saw Frank do it or snitched on him, as the next day he was called to Mr. Clossey's office, where he was told to bring his mother to school on the morrow. The next morning, Frank and his mother, who was one of the seamstresses employed in a shop in the Blanchard block, arrived as we gathered for classes. Soon they reappeared with Frank being dragged by his ear, his mother shouting at him as they ascended the hill and eventually disappeared from sight. We didn't find out until several days later that Frank's mother had to pay to replace the tree, something like $5.00, a goodly sum in those days, and that he was grounded. To top everything else off, he lost his jackknife, the ultimate insult.

The tree seemed to wilt for a short while, but eventually perked up and grew at an amazing rate, soon towering over the rest of the planted saplings. Frank always said that, since he had paid for the tree, he would come back sometime and cut it down. He never did and that tree stands tall and proud to this day. I suppose legally it does belong to the school but we, his contemporaries, always referred to it as Frank's tree.

About the time I was in the 7th grade, I discovered the Kellogg-Hubbard Library. At that time, we were studying the Civil War and we had to write a paper about it. So I went to the library, obtained a card and took out two books about the subject. With these as references, I wrote my paper and caught the Civil War bug. I took out book after book on the subject, particularly books on the individual battles. The story of Shiloh and its poignancy particularly affected me. This experience triggered my appreciation of books and reading that is still strong today. I discovered Sir Walter Scott, the tales of the Knights of the Round Table, Robert Louis Stevenson, and yes, even William Shakespeare. Whole worlds opened up to me amidst hours of enjoyment. I read the works of Kenneth Roberts and James Fennimore Cooper and became enthralled with the history of our country. These led me into reading all I could about the American Revolution, and enabled me to possess information that helped me immensely in future classes on these subjects.

32

In the fall of 1938, on a fine September day, reports of a large storm were issued from the weather bureau. A hurricane of some strength had crossed the Florida coast and was moving rapidly north up the eastern seaboard. It had already caused considerable damage to the Cape Hatteras area, and by mid-day was battering the coast of New Jersey. We were warned that, as it moved up the coast, we would have heavy rain in all of New England.

Sure enough, toward late afternoon clouds blackened the sky and soon rain was upon us. As the day changed into deep darkness, the rain came on gusts of wind in ever-increasing volume. By six o'clock in the evening, reports on the radio warned that the storm had passed New Jersey and had hit Connecticut and Massachusetts in full fury, then had turned directly north across Connecticut and the Berkshires of Massachusetts, and was heading straight for Vermont. The main path being projected was up the Connecticut River Valley. Since we were situated in Central Vermont and surrounded by the Green Mountains fully fifty miles from the valley, we were told and expected that we would experience only heavy rain.

As the night progressed, rain increased to become absolute cloudbursts, blocking vision beyond our street light in front of the house. About nine o'clock, all the lights went out and we were in perfect darkness. We lit kerosene lamps and candles in holders, and all us kids were sent to bed and left in the total black of night. Soon flashes of lightning lit up the scene as we watched through the windows of our bedrooms. Sleep became impossible as roaring wind and rolling thunder shook the house, sheets of rain thundering on the roofs and against the windowpanes.

Watching from our windows as the lightning played all over the sky, we could see the bend of the trees in the streets that fronted them. The lightning came in almost continual patterns, and you could see almost as well as by sunlight. Tree limbs were crashing into the streets. Above the tumult created by thunder, wind, and rain could be heard the sound of breaking trees.

As we watched, several trees on our street and Edwards Street were flattened, their roots torn out of the ground, taking phone and electrical wires with them crashing onto the street. We were terrified but strangely exhilarated by all we were seeing and hearing. After about an hour of watching, it seemed to calm down somewhat and the lightning became less frequent, although the rain came down as fiercely as before. Lulled by this calming effect and the return of total darkness, I fell asleep.

The next day there was not even talk of going to school as we surveyed the damage done by the storm. Light sprinkles of very gentle rain rippled the pools of water in holes washed out here and there on the street by the horrendous rain during the night. Trees that an adult could not put their arms around lay all over the neighborhood. Amazingly, although they lay across the streets, only one had struck a building, a garage used as a shed by one neighbor, crushed dead center of its length.

We were confined to our immediate property and not allowed in the streets, as wires were downed by fallen trees and no one knew which were live. During the course of several days, crews of men sawed up the downed trees and trucked the branches off. The remaining blocks of wood were rolled onto sidewalks or lawns for the owner's disposition. Electric and phone crews hung the wires back up, replacing poles damaged during the storm, and eventually lights and power, as well as phone service, were restored.

City crews worked on the washed-out streets and, as October approached, had repaired most of the damage. Remnants of the storm were still about in the form of broken tree limbs and downed trees on private property, some of which remained there for many years to come. Most lawns, especially those with banks, had landscaping to be done in the spring of the next year before complete normalcy was achieved. As far as I ever knew, no one was seriously injured, though property damage was widespread throughout the state.

After the clean up, we were again allowed to pursue our wandering ways and, of course, we headed for our favorite haunts. Sabin's Pasture and woods was one of the first places we raced to. The sight of almost the whole woodland flattened from a south to north direction greeted us. Trees lay either side by side or atop each other in an amazingly ordered fashion chosen by the direction of the hurricane winds that had uprooted them. We walked on the trunks, only temporarily held up by the foliated branches, all the way to the Montpelier Country Club, a distance of at least a mile, before having to climb down to ground level. The only trees that seemed to survive this onslaught were pines of less than thirty or forty feet in height and, strangely enough, the tall elms. Maple trees were especially vulnerable to the high winds, I suppose because of their large mass of leaf cover. The sugarbush suffered greatly and it was many years before it grew back to maturity.

We found out that the hurricane, which we had been told would follow the Connecticut River Valley, had instead swept directly up the Green Mountain chain. We were in its direct path. We have had, as a people, many disasters brought on by excessive weather of various kinds. The Flood of 1927, years during the early 1800's when crops failed because winter never ended, and other devastations in select areas, but no storm to date has had such a profound effect on the environment of the State of Vermont as the Hurricane of 1938, nor had such an impact on the people who lived through it, myself included. Sixty years has given the environment time to recover and all traces of this mighty blow are now gone from sight, but it still lives sharply in memory for those of us who saw it.

33

Being so recently removed from the customs of their native land, my family naturally observed New Year's as the prime holiday of "the old country" with all the fervor reserved for native sons and daughters of old Scotland. I was drawn to those activities most dear to my Scottish family and their acquaintances on this most important day. New Year's was of first importance to the Scots for two reasons, first being the hope, however faint, of better times ahead; and secondly, the excuse to loosen up from a rather sterile and stoic lifestyle by the ingestion of their beloved "Aqua Vita" or whiskey. The new immigrants celebrated the passing of the old year with heightened anticipation of change in the land of opportunity.

First Footing—the visiting of friends from house to house and an excuse for mutual libation—was observed, starting early on New Year's Eve and lasting through the entire day beyond. Although we children were much too young to actually join in the festivities, we were caught up in the enthusiasm of the celebration to the extent that we participated in devouring whatever non-alcoholic goodies of the day were available.

Valentine's Day was, as it is now, not a holiday, but only a day noted for communicating degrees of affection, a card or note, mostly homemade, with others. Lincoln's and Washington's birthdays were both school holidays celebrated by us with relief and play after spending days learning about the lives of these noted men. Independence Day, the Fourth of July, we celebrated enthusiastically the same way we do today.

Halloween was a day, or I should say night, when adults shuddered in fear of the damages they might suffer at the hands of children who used the event as an excuse for reprisal for real or imagined injury. To us, it was a small way to get revenge on those we did not like or respect. We did acts designed to infuriate our antagonists. We played pranks, such as throwing rotten vegetables to splatter on their porches or doorsteps, or distributing their carefully canned garbage about their pristine lawns. We removed steps made of wood and moved those objects we could handle to strange places. Those we liked or respected remained secure and untouched by impish hands. A few of these even called us into their homes for a glass of cider as we roamed the neighborhood, or gave us perhaps a doughnut or an apple or even the rare piece of candy. This was the precursor to today's trick or treat, although that thought had not entered our minds in those days. By the latter days of my childhood, parties were being planned in our city to keep the children from destructive behavior. I'm sad to say that, for the most part, we either ignored these overtures or used them as a base for our mischievous evening.

Thanksgiving was a big holiday of the time. In New England, it had been long celebrated as a school holiday with special emphasis on Pilgrim study and in Currier and Ives calendar prints of sleighs being driven to "Grandmother's House" over fields of snow. We celebrated for many years without the now-required turkey as our meal until the availability of the noble bird brought it to a reasonable price. Dressed birds could be obtained in those later days, but their price was prohibitive to all but the wealthy. I remember the dispatch of farmyard chickens on the day before the holiday. The local theater had a special matinee, usually a film portraying the Pilgrim times that we attended with our childish enthusiasm simply as a means of escaping the cleanup.

We also celebrated November 11th, Armistice Day, as the day World War I—known to us as the war to end all wars—ended, with speeches in front of City Hall and a parade through the main streets of the city. The minute of silence paid in tribute to those who never made it home was a solemn and feeling ceremony observed by all with proper decorum, children included. The only sound that broke that mutual moment was the sound of pigeon wings as they flew about the clock tower of City Hall. After the ceremonies of the 11th minute of the 11th hour of the 11th day of the 11th month, everyone returned home to eat lunch and, as we children became older, to head for the local football game between Montpelier and Spaulding played that afternoon. All in all, it was a full day.

Easter, aside from the boredom of church, was a Sunday like all Sundays with an occasional egg hunt in the fields that bounded the small lawns beside our house. We were compensated for the number of eggs we found with a given number of jelly beans handed out by our adult judges, a momentary excitement at best, before being allowed to return to our usual pursuits, and only on those rare years when the fields were not snow laden.

Christmas was the time looked forward to by us kids, not in anticipation of gifts, but rather as a break in our school routine. During and after the Great Depression, money was perhaps the scarcest commodity, so we knew that gifts would be practical if we got any at all. We expected that Christmas would bring such things as new winter underwear, socks, home knit mittens, scarves, and toques. It was also time for new Johnson pants, and high-cut boots. Our only hope was that we would be lucky enough to get those high-cuts that had a jack-knife in a pocket on the side of the boot.

Our stockings were hung in anticipation of Christmas candy, perhaps a couple of rolls of Lifesavers, a toothbrush and some fruit, maybe tangerines or an orange, and a few unshelled nuts. Once in a while, someone would wrap a game or two that we could all play with as family, or a puzzle made by a neighbor. I can't remember being disappointed, because we didn't anticipate toys or such to be to given us, although one Christmas we all got American Flyer sleds which brought much joy.

Mostly it was the school vacation we looked forward to and all the activities we knew we'd have time for—sliding, tobogganing, skiing and, if conditions were right, skating.

34

Most years, we would have had enough cold weather by Christmas vacation to freeze the Winooski River, if not under the Main Street Bridge, then at least down beyond the one on Granite Street. If it was deemed safe to skate on, the city would keep a large area just down from the bridge cleared by a horse-drawn wooden plow. Snow banks built up by plowing would enclose the area and serve as seats to rest on. An approach was cleared on the Granite Street side leading down the bank to the river. Crowds of both children and adults would appear on weekends, and the city provided a guard of sorts to keep the rink in order.

The hand-me-down skates we wore were given out by our families according to whatever size came close to fitting each individual. The criteria for fit were simple: if you could put your foot in the skate, it fit. I started out with a pair of tubular skates that might have been known as hockey skates. They had a boot that runners would be fit to that was wide and made of stiff leather. These suited me fine, since I hardly used the runners anyway while learning to skate. I spent most of the time on the inner sides of the leather portion of the skate. However, unskilled as I was, I really enjoyed trying, and had a good time stumbling around with my friends whose skill level was no greater than mine.

After a few years, the city decided to move skaters from the river. They built two rinks, one in the park on the meadow area and one at the campus of the Seminary. Skating on the river was then prohibited. So we shifted to the Seminary where horses with their special wood plows cleared a large area on the campus. The sides were built up and the rink flooded with a fire hose attached to hydrants at the corner of College and East State Streets. The flooding usually took place at night on the coldest nights possible to ensure proper ice build-up. Steam would rise from the water while it was in the act of freezing and cloud the rink. Under a pale moon in a cloudless sky, it made for a strange, eerie scene on the snow-covered winter campus.

At times, they built a sort of tower of two by fours and strung a series of lights from a pole on East State Street that bisected the rink for night skating. The lights were only lit on Friday and Saturday nights, so we skated either by moonlight or blindly in snowstorms on weeknights. Due to the campus' close proximity to our house, we usually put our skates on at home and walked to the rink.

This wore the edges down, as well as our leg muscles. Every two or three weeks, we had to take our skates downtown where Mr. Mossier sharpened them in his shoe repair shop for ten cents a pair.

By this time, I had acquired a pair of tight figure skates that I could skate on, although they hurt my feet. Because of the tight fit, I could wear but one layer of socks. My feet froze to the point where there was usually little feeling left except for the extreme cold. I would arrive home after skating, peel off the skates and socks, and stick my club-like feet in a bowl of warm water until the feeling came back, sometimes with extreme pain. It is a wonder that I didn't lose some toes to frostbite, for their color was absolutely white when I removed my skates.

By the time I was twelve years old, I had skated enough by watching adults and mimicking their moves to figure skate quite well, and won my first trophy in competition. I could do figure eight's, the vine, and simple reverse jumps, as well as reversing rolls where you change edges without raising your one foot off the ice. Skating became very important to me as a winter sport, until I ran into and knocked down a girl one night. Then for some reason I became more interested in the girl than the sport.

35

The sounds and smells of life in the 1930's were quite different from what we hear and smell today. When we heard a saw, for instance, it was either the sound of a carpenter's hand saw or a cross-cut limb saw, or even the putt-putt of a jacked up Model-A with a belt attached to a circular wood cutting disc saw. It was not the raucous, full-throated roar of a chainsaw that now permeates the landscape. When a truck or piece of road equipment backed up, it sounded the same as if it was going forward in low gear, not like today when an electronic beep sends its annoying shriek to assail your ears.

In winter, the gentle tinkling of sleigh bells often took your notice as someone paced his horse up a road or street. The lonely wail of the steam train reverberated in the valleys with long whooshing sounds that made you feel comforted by its presence. Today, though some trains still run that comforting wail, most have been replaced by a blatant blast that, if unexpected, jolts your senses.

Trains at that time tracked most of the valleys of Vermont with main lines. The Barre-Montpelier railway had additional spurs to the granite quarries and to Williamstown. The Montpelier-Wells River ran from Montpelier through East Montpelier, Plainfield and on through Groton Forest to Wells River, where it joined the Canadian main line down the Connecticut River to White River Junction. Numerous spurs of these and the main lines served many small towns. Trains were the main form of transporting freight. Many of the roads were still graveled, and quite a few of the main roads had not been paved. So I grew up with the belching monsters of those rails, with their coal-fired smoke pouring from black chimneys, roaring down the tracks, and frequently heard their whistle as they approached some crossing along the way.

Even when far from the tracks, that mournful wail would sound up the ridges to us as we hunted or hiked the mountains that looked down on them. Walking the railroad bed was always a danger, though we could tell when a train was coming because the tracks would vibrate. By putting an ear to them you could tell how far away they were and get off the bed before the train raced by, spewing hot cinders down on you. Walking the bridges was scarier, since there was nowhere to go if caught on them, so we raced across as fast as we could.

The sound of steel horseshoes on cobbled streets and the metal rims of the wagons they pulled are gone forever from the valley where I grew up. The clip-clop of the milk wagon in the dark of early morning, and the occasional whinny of the horses that drew them and the other carriages is also lost. I say these things not to criticize or critique today, but out of feelings of nostalgia for my own past and because, even if I tried, I could not expunge my memory of them.

The way things were done and how we looked was all so different then. I remember sawdust spread on the floors of the markets, mainly to absorb the mud tracked in from dirt and granite dust streets after or during a rain shower. Even the national chains—A & P and Grand Union—spread sawdust thickly so that you tread on it on damp days.

Anywhere outside the cities and municipal areas, the kerosene lamp was the main source of illumination in farmhouses and barns. The Rural Electrification Administration (REA) of the Roosevelt New Deal Program was just starting to provide electricity to these rural areas in the mid-1930's, and the Co-ops of today were just being born. Homes were heated with either wood or coal, and the most popular system was hot air, usually with a large central register cut into the first floor level, augmented by ducts that led to smaller registers in the other rooms of the first floor. Any heat that rose above the first floor, either through open stair-ways or small registers cut into second floors, quickly dissipated when mixed with the cold air penetrating through uninsulated walls or faulty windows. Although the wooden storm windows were put on over the existing windows, on cold mornings the frost would build up to where you could not see out. As the weather warmed during the day, the frost would melt to pool inside the window-sills.

Our clothing as we grew was mostly hand-me-downs from family or friends of the adults in our family. Hand-me-downs for both males and females were common practice in those days, and you wore with pride whatever garment you were lucky enough to receive. Often the garment had to be re-tailored in order to fit, and jackets, pants, dresses, and coats were constantly changing shape within families. My first pair of pants, other than shorts for summer wear or Johnson pants in winter, were a pair of golf knickers. Knickers were built like shorts that extended below the knees, with the bottoms designed to clasp tightly below the knees where the calves began. They were either elasticized or snapped over folds of material. Mine were the snap kind in a brown and white check. I was not alone in wearing them, as many of the children at that time also did. Usually you wore long stockings that came up just below the knee to be covered by the knickers bottoms. It was not until the seventh or eighth grade that we were allowed to wear long pants, made mostly of denim, or as we called them, "overall" pants. Also, lucky for me, by that time I had grown enough that I could wear some of Victor's cast-off pants, mainly to school. I had had a suit when I was young that was worn only on special occasions such as Easter, but that was when my father was still with us. I quickly outgrew the suit and Mother couldn't afford to buy many clothes from that time on.

Men wore hats called fedoras, with a slight downward turn of the brim over the eyes. No man was completely dressed in all his finery unless he wore his fedora. In summer months, this was put on a closet shelf to repose until fall, and they got out their summer straw hats. These were actually made of thick straw, formed with a short, flat-topped body surrounded by a brim, perhaps three inches wide, that projected at right angles to the body. You could tell the season by seeing which hat men wore.

When I was quite young, I had a set of lead soldiers, all shaped in different positions depicting the doughboys of World War I. I played with them for hours at a time, setting them up in positions my imagination would suppose to be actual activity during the war. Outdoors, I would make trenches in the ground, and with small sticks set up fortifications resembling the trench warfare of France and Belgium. In the set were several cannon and caissons meant to look like the horse-drawn weapons of that era, as well as ambulances and tanks, all made of lead. If one believes the warnings of lead usage today, I'm lucky to be alive, as I chewed those soldiers' heads off, and am sure my quota of lead must have been a fatal dosage by today's standards. We also had lead statuary depicting cowboys and Indians that were afforded the same treatment, as well as cars and trucks and numerous other toys made of that dreaded poison. I sometimes reflect on the fact that, had I not been exposed to all that lead, I would undoubtedly have been a genius with unlimited mental capacity.

36

Victor's father, as well as being in the cattle business, had a string of trotting horses that he raced at all the best tracks along the eastern seaboard. He had even raced in the Hamiltonian Stakes, the premier event in trotting. I used to help him harness up for practice runs and watch him pace the short ring behind his house. In later years, after Vic's father's death, Victor took over the harness racing. Today his son Michael races in fairs all around New England.

Victor also liked to ride horseback, and kept riding horses for many years. One summer, he acquired a pinto pony taken in trade for cattle. He brought the pony down to our house on Foster Street one Saturday and saddled it up. We kids took turns riding it up and down the street. Victor decided, because of my size, that I should ride him more than the others. So for that summer and the next, I rode quite often at the farm on Trow Hill. The pasture Victor used was across the intersection and down a short way, adjacent to Donald Smith's apple orchard. I would ride to the gate, open it, and drive the milk cows he had in the pasture to the barn like a regular cowboy. Of course, I had to unsaddle the pony, rub him down, give him grain, water, and hay, and polish up the saddle and tack, as well as help with the cow chores. It was still fun and I enjoyed my only experience with horseback riding.

When my family—that is Father, Mother, and I—lived on Ayers Street in Barre, we were directly across the street from the old Barre Fairgrounds. An oval track covered most of the land with a grandstand that backed the river. At that time, the Civilian Conservation Corps was using the land as an encampment. Large tents dotted much of the area, with a stable of sorts along the riverbank, from the street to the grandstand. Horses and mules used in their projects were stabled there. Even a small building set off by itself, which held the dynamite and blasting powder, was included in this temporary settlement.

My father had a drinking acquaintance, one of the sergeants stationed there. I got guided tours to most of the tents, cook tents, and stables, as well as an underground food storage vault. This was where the men who built the huge East Barre Dam slept and ate. It was a very sparse existence at best. There were no luxuries evident, except for the main commodity of men in those times—liquor.

My father had a friend—an Italian gentleman—smaller in stature than even he, a friendly man with a quick smile and quiet demeanor. He and his wife were childless and both doted on me when I was brought to visit them. Her name escapes my memory and I only remember him by his first name, Silvio. He made much of me and talked to me, which other adults did not do. The first time I ever saw them was when Mother and Father visited them on their small farm in Plainfield. I was particularly impressed with all the small animals—dogs, cats, chickens, and even two young calves, which I tried but failed to catch.

We stayed the afternoon and were invited to supper with them. My father and I followed Silvio through the kerosene-lit kitchen into a shed attached behind. There hung a huge quarter of frozen meat. Silvio had been hunting in Quebec and had bagged a moose, which he had brought back. I remember vividly his cutting steaks with a large butcher knife, seeing the partially iced meat showing crystals in the lamplight.

The only other memory of Silvio I have is of him in a satin-lined casket with a picture of a man's face over a pierced heart. I was told he was dead, but at that time, death did not mean anything to me. I supposed that Silvio was sleeping and that everyone was being quiet so as not to awaken him. I found out much later in life that he had died of silicosis, as had my Grandfather Ewen.

37

The Sykas family moved to Foster Street from Barre in the late 1930's, three houses down the street from us. Mr. William, the father, I recalled from my days in Barre. Jim, the oldest son, was much older than us kids. He was a junior or senior in high school, so we were not exposed much to him at that time. Tom, the second oldest, was a large boy with a jolly disposition close in age to my aunt Buddy. John was a couple of years older, but closer in age to us, more serious in temperament, but friendly enough to be included. Peter was a couple of years younger than I was and he fit in fine. Paul had yet to be born, and I only knew him as Peter's younger brother as we were growing up. Tom we saw a lot of, as he liked to hang around our back porch and talk with Buddy and, although older than us, often joined in our games or talked to us.

One day as it was gently raining, we gathered on our spacious porch just yapping about things in general. Tom was in his usual position sitting on the porch railing. Suddenly there was a loud crack, and both the railing and Tom fell slowly backward, disappearing from sight. Tom at that time probably weighed close to two hundred pounds and had been warned repeatedly about sitting on the railing. The height from the ground was about twelve feet. We all rushed off the porch to see if he was badly injured.

Down the outside stairs we tore to find Tom flat on his back with his legs entangled in the railing. He could not speak for a short while because landing had knocked the breath out of him. In a couple of minutes, he began to breathe better and moved to get to his feet. We pulled the railing away from him and he rose. The only complaint he had was that his back hurt a little. We made our way back to the porch, where he stretched out on an old day bed and protested that he was all right. After a while, he got up and went home, saying again that he was fine and none the worse for his fall. As the years went by, I took note of the fact that Tom always had a problem with his back, and have remained convinced that his bad back was a direct result of this fall.

We got along with all the Sykases, played our games with them, became friends, and in later years were always friendly even though we followed different paths. In fact, I introduced John's wife to him, and as adults Peter and his family used to play cards and socialize with us. Our sons later became good friends.

Curiosity about the steep hills that rose from the narrow flats by the branches of the Winooski River drove us to climb them and look down on the valley where we lived. There were four main promontories that surrounded us. Hubbard Park with its stone tower lay behind the State House. Clay Hill or Towne Hill Road rose above Seminary Hill to the northeast. To the south was what we called Berlin Hill or Prospect Hill. The top of North Street towered over Elm Street and the North Branch Valley. To climb three of these, we needed only to walk the roads that led to their tops. The other, Prospect Hill, we reached by starting at Jim Slack's house part way up Hill Street, which we crossed, then passed into the steep pasture beyond. After a hard climb over cow paths that crossed the precipitous pasture, we reached the top, which was a narrow strip of maple woods that crowned the hill. From there, the best and most panoramic view of the city of Montpelier was spread before us. We looked down across the valley to puny Seminary Hill well underneath our perch. We looked across to the tops of both North Street and Towne Hill Road, and Hubbard Tower topping Hubbard Park below. I had never realized just how tightly the city wrapped itself within the ridges that surrounded it, and with the view came the realization of how small it really was.

On one memorable day, Peter and John Sykas and I decided to climb the Hubbard Park Tower on our way home from a ballgame. We wound our way up the curving roads leading to the tower with frequent stops until we crested that rise of ledge that marks the top of Hubbard Park hill. Although Hubbard Park encompassed a high and at one point precipitous hill rising behind the State Capital building, it is looked down upon by the other ridges that surround the City of Montpelier. Its view from the tower in the 1930's showed most areas of downtown Montpelier, particularly that portion below Seminary Hill that was formed by the Winooski River Basin. The trees that now block most of that view were just saplings and were, with the exception of the many elms that towered on both sides of most Montpelier streets, the only ones noticeable from the park. One could follow the course of Main Street as it wended its way to the Kinstead bend, and College Street leading across the ridge to the Seminary whose campus was visible, as well as its tall administration building. Parts of other streets such as East State Street showed clearly and the Primary School as well as Washington Grammar School could be spotted readily.

Looking down on the State House dome, shining brilliant gold under the statue of Ceres, the Goddess of Agriculture, and over the tops of the elms that lined State Street, the river meandered and the National Life field spread almost to the mouth of the Dog River before one's eyes. Looking to the left, the ridge across the North Branch of the Winooski River was almost nude of vegetation, with open pasture around its perimeter, touching the Catholic Cemetery and the Kinstead lands beyond. In short, it was a pleasant and entertaining view of the area.

We climbed the steel steps that lined the inside of the stone-built tower slowly due to the tiredness of our legs and my fear of tall buildings. Viewed from the base, the edifice did not seem any higher than a three story house, and its width was about the size of a large room in most homes of today, its inner dimensions about fourteen or fifteen feet across. I still shuddered, weak-kneed as I paced up the stairs. Arriving at the top platform where the sides rose between four and five feet, I cautiously and with extreme trepidation stood, climbing the inner stones, with arms across the palisade formed by the top layer to see the view. Shorter Peter and taller John, meanwhile, hoisted their butts to perch sidesaddle on the top of the stone as if sitting a stone fence in a field.

As we marveled at the wide views before us, John suggested we climb the stones from the base on the outside of the tower. Peter and I shouted down that idea. Instead, we decided that because of the lateness of the day we should make our way home. The light was beginning to fade as the sun slanted in the west. We made our way down the stairs, climbed the wall that surrounds the base, and walked around the top. As we were doing this, we noticed a change in the light. Glancing down the valley, we saw the sun setting between dark clouds, appearing like a red ball. Now the whole atmosphere seemed to have a bronze-red cast. Even the light and dark greens of the tree foliage glowed with this strange color.

We made our way back up the tower and could discern all we had viewed before changed and subtly changing further as we watched. All the hills, buildings, and foliage darkened by stages to almost blood red. Even the Montpelier semi-pro baseball team playing at the National Life Field took on these shades of color as they stood or ran in the machinations of the game. Our faces as we spoke to each other were red as though from embarrassment. Everything in view except that portion of the sky which had shadowed to an almost pale orange color was the same, distinguishable only by its shading. We watched spellbound for some time until the sun sank into that bank of clouds and twilight returned.

We left the park in the waning light of day and by strenuous running made it home as the streetlight's faint glow was appearing. I just made the kitchen as supper was served and listened to the usual harangue, "Where have you been?" I tried in my usual manner to explain our fascination only to be met by their customary disinterest and the usual admonishments of "Don't be late again!" and other comments known to all errant children.

I have witnessed this phenomenon but a few times in my life but never has it been as vivid or exciting as it was that day. Nobody seemed to care about my experience, but I did, and with sharp memory still do.

38

One night in the month of October, Shelly Miller and I decided to watch for falling stars and the northern lights. The weather had been exceedingly warm—unusual that late in the month. Daytime temperatures under clear blue skies had reached the low 80's that day and, even with the sinking of the sun in the west, a balmy evening was in store. Two or three nights previously, we had lain on our backs on the Seminary campus opposite his home and seen a few falling stars and a vivid display of northern lights that had, by late evening, covered most of our segment of the night sky.

We lay on our backs staring up at a sky deep black with a myriad of stars that glistened with varying light. We discussed the position of constellations, and had a really clear view of the Milky Way that filmed across the star-studded sky before us. No displays of the northern lights lit the sky as we watched, but an occasional falling star streaked a thread-like trail, breaking the pattern of the night. No moon showed, and the few lights on the perimeter of campus did not interfere nor penetrate the darkness.

We had just discussed the stars in Orion when a bright greenish light appeared to our north. As it crossed the sky, it left a tail of some length behind it and changed color to yellow and red as it raced to the west. Probably only seconds elapsed, but to us it seemed to hang in the sky for an amazing period of time. Then it disappeared as swiftly as it had appeared. Shelly said it had to be a meteor, as a comet would not disappear so suddenly. We rose from the ground and raced back to his house to tell his father what we had seen.

Webb Miller, Shelley's father, was District Attorney, a learned man with imposing countenance and bushy eyebrows like his namesake, Daniel Webster. Mr. Miller was also one of a group that called itself "The Club", an organization devoted to the arts and sciences. He was a member of the National Geographic Society as well. When we told him what we had seen, he questioned us extensively about its colors, the direction of its flight and the intensity of light of the object. Concluding that what we had witnessed was a meteorite passing through the earth's atmosphere, he said he would follow up on it. The next day, he called the Society and reported what we had seen.

A couple of weeks later, Mr. Miller called me while I was eating supper to see if I could come to his house. When I arrived, I found Mr. Miller and Shelly with two other men waiting for me. It seems the two men were from Washington, DC, the headquarters of the National Geographic Society. They were there to question Shelly and me about the meteorite. After taking down our statements about what we had seen, they informed us it was indeed a meteorite, and that it had struck the earth in Kansas in a farmer's field. They had pictures and samples of rock from it, which they showed us.

They explained that the changing colors we had seen were different elements in the meteorite being burned off by the heat of friction produced by our atmosphere's resistance to its flight. They also said it was a rather large one, for after it struck the earth, it still was several feet in circumference and weighed about two tons. After several months, Mr. Miller showed us an article about the meteorite in the National Geographic Magazine, which gave full credit to Shelly and me as the only eyewitnesses they could find of the event.

39

One day I woke to a sun that shone brightly on a new coating of fresh snow measuring about 3 inches, adding to the layers to total about 14 or 15 inches on the ground. It was a perfect day for the skiing trip we had planned. My companions for this venture were Shelley Miller, Pete Sykas and Fuzz Taylor, two older and one younger than I. Shelley, the oldest, was our leader and had proposed the trip. From his back porch, he spied a house facing him in the far distance up the north branch valley. This house, it turned out, was situated at the lower end of the Horn of the Moon region of East Montpelier. Our plan was to go cross-country, up Main Street, across the Murray farm and follow the ridge formed between Main and North Streets to the Harpan farm, thence down through woods of the "Moon" to our destination.

We started at about 9:00 a.m. at Shelley's house across from the Seminary Campus and headed up College Street to where it joins Main Street. Shelley, Pete, and Fuzz had just acquired new ski harnesses made of leather that strapped their boots in tightly. I was still using Ball jar rubbers looped over the toe of my boots, around the bootstrap and around the heel.

The first part of our trek went well, as we were skiing on roads and across open fields, stopping only for fences where we had to undo our harnesses and redo them again when we had crossed the barbed wire. Despite the new snow and the warm temperature at our start, we had waxed our skis well, so we had little problem maneuvering through the fields. We were all wearing wool clothing, the ultimate in winter gear at the time, which aside from being unwieldy was also warm beneath its bulk. My outfit consisted of long underwear covered by wool pants stuffed into heavy wool socks that filled my boots to tighten their clasp on my feet. My upper clothing consisted of a wool flannel shirt worn under a heavy wool sweater, which was in turn covered with a light parka with no lining. A wool toque topped my head and partially covered my ears, and wool gloves covered my hands. We crossed the fields on the side of the extension of North Street, where jackets were taken off and tied about our waists as sweat began to flow from our exertions and the warmth of that morning sun. I was getting uncomfortable as the sweat built and had shed my sweater, as well as my jacket.

We entered the spruces and balsams beyond the open fields and fought our way down and up hogbacks still littered with the blow-down of the '38 hurricane. Several times we had to backtrack in search of better routes when huge trees or tops blown down stymied us. All this exertion soaked our remaining clothes. We neared our destination, climbing uphill to the road from a deep ravine through which, in warmer times, a brook flowed, now ice covered. My ski lodged under a concealed limb and I kept going, only to pitch full body forward to fall flat on my face in the snow. This broke my jar rubber and had to be replaced. The others started their climb as I hurried to join them.

I started to cross the brook in Shelley's tracks when the ice collapsed beneath me, and skis, boots and lower legs plunged into icy water. On feeling the icy water fill my boots, I struggled mightily to free myself and continued up the steep, precipitous side of the hill ahead. We reached the top and entered the snow-covered road, spying our house across the road and up a slight rise in front of us.

As the others sat on the snow bank formed by the plows that occasionally cleared the roadway and reached for their sandwiches from their jacket pockets, I sat and removed my boots. The soaked ski boots were short, barely covering the ankles and had a hard square toe with no lining. I took my socks off, one at a time, and wrung the water out as best I could, replacing them and shoving them back into the now damp leather to conserve what warmth I could. In truth, they still retained some body warmth at that moment.

We ate our lunch discussing the events of the day so far, ending with the plan of our return. All agreed that to return by following our tracks through the hell of blow downs we had penetrated in getting here was foolish and that we would take an alternate route home. Not knowing the lay of the land around us, nor knowing that we were but a short distance from the Worcester road and just above the town dump, we decided we would return by slabbing the side of the ridge until we struck North Street. Once there, it would be all down hill to Main Street, then across to Loomis, up Liberty crossing on Hubbard to East State Street, then up to the Seminary. Little did we know that although plausible, it was by far the furthest route.

Shelley had a watch that he consulted, showing the time to be 1:30 p.m. Since this was a late December day, we knew sundown was about 4:30 p.m., giving us three hours of light to make the trek. Although the sun had faded, leaving a leaden gray sky and the temperature dropping somewhat, we gave no thought to how cold it might become, though all donned their jackets before our start.

We cut back down the steep bank, crossed the brook and climbed the next hogback, then down its declivity on its other side, only to face another rise. In this manner, we plodded on, having to adjust for the usual blow downs and copses of thick spruce along our way. Gently, at first from our right, which faced the North Branch Valley, the wind seemed to freshen, and tendrils of blowing snow, exacerbated by falling loads from the tree branches above us, rose to obscure our vision. I was well aware of the dropping temperature and the cold seeping through my clothing, particularly those cold, wet socks and boots. We finally found ourselves on the edge of open fields at the top of North Street, where we were greeted by blowing snow and cold winds that swept the open space just as the daylight of day left us. By then, all jackets had been pulled tight, and toques were adjusted to cover ears being bitten by that sharp cold that appears as darkness falls. Small twinges of panic prevailed upon us as the horizon disappeared into the gathering darkness that seemed to suck the last warmth on earth within its vastness.

My feet and lower legs had become club-like and were so cold they had even ceased to ache from the chill. By now, even the part between my cuffs and gloves were frozen and my wrists hurt with that biting chill that heralds frostbite.

We skied across the flat field into the slight depression of the road and followed it across the open until we reached the city line. There we found, to our chagrin that the city had plowed to the line. This meant we had to ski down that steep grade on the shoulders formed by the snow thrown up by the snowplow. Because of the precipitous nature of North Street, it was a problem made worse by barbed wire fences that lined the roadway and left only a narrow space on which to ski. The plowed surface of the road, windswept for several hours, was icy and hard, making it impossible to control our descent. We proceeded cautiously in a staggered line to allow for the person in front to adjust, sometimes on the top of the snow bank. Other times, the fence posts appeared in our ski line and we had to brake, putting us on the icy road where we poled fiercely to stay erect.

With the extreme discomfort of my frozen feet, the others soon left me behind. Then the ultimate horror struck as another jar rubber broke and that ski rocketed down the hill ahead of me. There was little I could do until I found the ski, so I removed the other, slinging it and my poles over a shoulder. I proceeded down the icy road edge on my clubfeet, keeping one boot in the snow bank for surer footing. Luckily, I found my ski after about 50 yards partially stuck in the snow bank, which was the good part. The bad part was that not only was the jar rubber gone, but also one side of the leather strap had broken off at the same time. In a frenzy of despair, I added the ski to my shoulder collection and plodded on down the hill.

By now, unadulterated agony had me in its grasp, accentuated by each step I took. Although the wind had died, the cold penetrated my whole body, especially where exposed. My wrists between glove and sleeve became more exposed as I struggled with the skis and poles on my shoulder and my face and ears stung in the bitter air. I kept adjusting my toque to no avail, as it seemed to ride up my head with each pace I took.

I wish I could say that the others in their concern awaited me at the foot of North Street, but when I arrived, there I was, still alone. With some chagrin, the fact dawned on me that they had deserted me to my fate and gone home to escape the deepening cold. How I made it I'll never know, aware only of the intense cold that invaded all parts of my body. I dimly recall passing streetlights marking the corners of the streets and the dark of the seminary campus as I crossed it.

Stacking my poles and skis in the corner of the back porch, I entered into a world of warmth in our kitchen. Hands swiftly stripped my boots, socks and clothes and wrapped a blanket about me. I shivered and chattered as I tried to tell my tale of the day. Hot water in a large basin was brought and my feet forced in. The agony of thawing out brought tears rolling down my still cold face as those two cold white appendages burned incessantly, cramping my arches. Hot chocolate was administered by one of my aunts and slowly the warmth penetrated, overwhelming that deep cold and magically making it disappear. After about an hour, I seemed to be back to normal and could relate my tale, after which I was hustled to a hot bath, then fed supper, after which I was sent directly to bed.

40

When I was about eleven or twelve, the new mode of transportation for us kids became the bicycle, with the balloon tires that are rarities today. Most of us could not afford to buy new bikes, but scrounged the dumps for discards. I was fortunate enough to find a full frame in one of my exploratory hunts and, although it was twisted, I assume by being run over, I dragged it home. With the help of my neighbors, I put together a bicycle. The blacksmith straightened the frame, so all I needed were the wheels, since the chain was still attached to the pedal sprocket when I found it. I repainted the frame and, after much more scrounging, found a front wheel that fit. The back wheel's sprockets and fenders were still missing, but by luck a friend came up with a serviceable back wheel. Rain, however, presented a problem as mud, sand, and water sprayed me front and back whenever I rode it. Although I couldn't find fenders, I managed to make do as it was. By buying new tires and inner tubes, I was in business, and could ride everywhere I chose. I could now transport myself to fishing places or to the municipal pool. I had no chain guard, so I used U-shaped bicycle clips made of spring metal that fit over tucked pant legs to keep them clear of the revolving chain. It was a jerry-rigged affair, but it served me well for several summers of pedaling adventure.

This method of saving and recycling was all pervasive in my youth, perhaps because of the Great Depression or just Yankee upbringing. Garbage itself was not garbage until declared spoiled beyond human ingestion and anything that had a possible use was used.

Most store packaging consisted of plain brown or white paper arranged on large rolls beside the cash register or beneath the counter on a shelf. Cast iron or steel fittings allowed one to pull the paper to the desired length and then tear it on a bar. Whatever was purchased was wrapped in paper and trussed in crossed formation by strings of different tensile strengths. Those of the butcher shop, in particular, were of stronger string and held heavy weights better than those strings used by dry goods merchants. These were prized, carefully unknotted, and wrapped around other lengths of the same weight in the form of balls, some of which grew to the size of soccer balls. These were used in turn to truss up chickens or turkeys after being stuffed. Several lengths together served as a sort of trellis, suspended by spaced poles, for growing beans and other vegetables to cling to in gardens. These stout strings were almost of cord size. Other lesser strings were wrapped in balls for whatever uses one needed and stored in drawers or cupboards about the house.

During the Christmas season, cords and strings of various colors were wrapped in like balls for use the next year. Ribbon from packages was accorded drawer space and separated by color for re-use, according to width and length.

Some foods were packaged in tins, cans, and boxes and others in various types of foils, mostly with a lead base. As these were taken off the products, they would be added to others in the standard ball shape. To what purpose this was done, I never really understood.

Pencils worn to a stub were saved if the erasers still had form enough to be used, and all manner of fountain pens, dried of their ink, rattled side by side in drawers, nesting with short lengths of unused yarn and used rubber bands that entangled all within. Perhaps the strangest treasures one would come across in a drawer search were those clothespins, minus the center spring, that reposed in clumps, saved for what use I never could fathom. Mechanical pencils in assorted shapes and sizes rolled about in those drawers awaiting lead reloads that somehow never materialized.

Paper, apparently unsoiled, lay in crumpled sheets stacked in a cupboard and folded to size. Various colors greeted the eye—the pale blue and brown of the druggist, the beige and occasionally striped white for the clothier, the distinctive off-white egg-shell or bland white of the grocer, standing in stacks weighed down by a heavy plate or bowl. Within the bottom doors of our fragrant china cupboard were the Christmas and birthday tissue paper that had wrapped previous gifts and only waited future occasion for re-use.

Pickle jars and discarded mayonnaise or salad dressing bottles, washed out and dried, were stacked in peach baskets and stored on the floor of our cellar storage room for pickling. Even used cans of various sizes, partially filled with dirt, awaited spring seedlings to be left before the lone window to mature before replanting in our garden. Anything that could be re-used was and was treasured by hoarding hands.

String is now something we rarely use. If needed, we purchase it in rolls of 100 feet or more. Lead foil is only used in certain containers of materials not intended for public use and we would recoil in horror at anyone's keeping it today, since most things are of a disposable nature in today's society.

41

"Write if you find work." The expression sums up the plights and trials of the depression years of the nineteen thirties. It is remembered by those of us who lived through it, bringing back stark and real memories of that bygone era.

Today we speak of unemployment as a state only dire when applied to those of the homeless. Being unemployed today can convey a loss of luxury but supported by all the agencies and programs designed to secure, at the least, a livable existence. Unemployed today can even be thought of as a vacation from toil, bringing with it a slight depression in buying power.

During those long and desperate days, it meant much more than a loss of spirit. It meant total and absolute poverty, only staved off by the occasional charity of other individuals. Families were diminished through necessity as members left home so that those left behind could have at least a modicum of sustainable existence. This was the time of itinerant wanderers who approached each farm or town with hope of some sort of employment and the opportunity to better oneself, hoping for a wood pile to be split or temporary work in the fields of the secure farmers, hoping to obtain a meal or board for a period of time.

There are many stories of that age that tell equally of the charity of some and the brutality of others they chanced upon. Some railroad workers would beat these travelers if they were found on their cars, where others looked the other way in compassion. Some people welcomed them in charity, where others turned them away as they enjoyed their own abundance. Human character showed itself in many ways.

Men who lost their jobs left home and family in the hope of finding employment elsewhere. If found, they would send word for the family to join them. Those at the send off uttered the statement "Write if you find work" with fervent prayer.

We now use this phrase in jest when one or the other of us leaves the house on some mundane errand such as getting the mail, taking out the garbage or leaving for a haircut. We mean no disrespect by doing this. In fact, by doing this, we bring back memories of those past days. I am sure that those hearing us express this saying do not know why we say it or have any idea of its import. You had to experience it at that time to appreciate its essence and importance in our lives.

42

Meals during the depression and during the war were governed with certain and unrelenting rules. Due to shortages of many commodities as well as funds to purchase them, definite problems arose within almost all households. There were a wide variety of methods used to stretch an almost non-existent budget quite common in those times.

Cereals popular at that time were few and standardized into only three categories: oatmeal, Cream of Wheat, and granulated wheat. Oatmeal was the Scots' preference, as it was the gruel or porridge of the "old country" where it was used at all meals when available, eaten as a staple with garnishment of salt; hence the expression I heard from the elder Scots of, "Nae sugar yer porridge–saut it!" We did not salt it, but consumed it with milk and what sugar we were allowed. Our ration of sugar was one level teaspoon even before wartime rationing made it even scarcer. Once or twice a week we were allowed, by consensus, a choice of Cream of Wheat or Wheatena. I learned to rise early to have first crack at the milk bottle that still had some residue of cream left from when it was removed with the cream spoon. Those that followed had only vestiges of "fatted milk" as I carefully decanted all I could for my meal.

Peanut butter, a fairly new commodity, and assorted jams or jellies sufficed for lunch, spread thinly on homemade bread and accompanied by a glass of milk, replaced with Kool-Aid on occasion during the heat of summer.

Tuna fish of the darkest variety was a cheap item, as was salmon canned with little care or discretion. On occasion we were fed what would now be considered a cheap grade of cat food that we, in our ignorance, considered a luxury. A mix of lettuce and mayonnaise help to disguise our fare.

Hamburg, being another inexpensive source of protein, was used frequently, but rarely made into patties. When it was made into patties, it was enriched with dried breadcrumbs to fill out its mass. Usually it was served as a portion of such gourmet delights as American Chop Suey, a concoction of noodles, tomatoes, and onions sparsely sprinkled with the sautéed meat, or Hungarian Goulash, a somewhat thicker mess of the same ingredients cooked longer with some mysterious herbal or seasoned base.

I would be remiss if I did not admit that we did, on occasion, have such fare as tough pork chops or equally stringy cubed steak, interspersed with the forever welcome fried chicken done to perfection. I would also be wrong not to mention such gastronomic delicacies as pickled tripe, fried squid, and "potted head," a gelatinous mix of pieces of pork or mutton flavored by beef bouillon cubes and served cold. Pork or beef liver was also cheap in those times and therefore frequent fare at evening meals.

All the above were served to us with constant reminders of our plight, such as, "You're lucky to have anything to eat," "Eat it all or no dessert," "It's good for you," or the greatest philosophical statement of the time, "People are starving in Europe!" This last statement caused me considerable thought and I mulled it over many times. I questioned (to myself), what did my eating have to do with "people starving in Europe? And if I did not eat, would it affect their status one iota? What I did not eat was not whisked from my plate for transport to Europe, nor did my ingestion of food fatten those starving children. However, I did know that our garbage went to Mr. Bohannon, our egg deliveryman, to feed his pigs–recycling in its purest form. As I became older, I realized it was a variation of the "you are lucky" statement put in a different way, but have always had twinges of conscience when I think back to that time.

43

About this same time, the style for my peers and me was to acquire an old fedora and, instead of using the snap-brim in the conventional way, push it up and hold it in place with a hairpin through the brim. It gave us the look of the western troopers seen in the many western movies we watched. If you didn't have such a hat, you were not, as they said at a later date, "cool" and therefore, were not with the "in" crowd.

The movies influenced our lives tremendously. One particular character of the serials shown before the main feature was The Spider, not to be confused with the later comic book character. This man was evil incarnate, and only a shadowy figure on the black and white movie screen. You would only glimpse his shadow in the midst of a terrifying night. He wore the requisite fedora and a MacIntosh raincoat with the collar turned up. One leg dragged and scraped the cobbled stones of the city streets he prowled. You never saw his face, just a shadow profile, as he clubbed his victims in the pitch dark between streetlights. Each episode, another victim would fall prey to him and, just before death, be illuminated by the flashlight he carried, which showed a spider web on the victim's features.

One night I was about to cross the back campus of Vermont College under a scudding, cloudy sky from which a pale moon showed only glimpses of light. It was in the fall of the year and a warm autumnal wind was briskly stirring fallen leaves about the ground, rattling bare branches in the denuded trees. All in all it was a very spooky night.

As I entered the path worn diagonally across the field, a figure detached itself from a large tree trunk. There he was—hat, coat, club, and flashlight, dragging a leg through the downed leaves. I swear I went straight up in the air, feet churning even before I came down and shot along the path. As I sped down the path, I heard a laugh behind me, and then Jim Seivwright's voice. As I stopped and turned, he approached laughing. I could make out his features in the moonlight that showed clearly at just that moment. My heart was racing. I shook as he handed me my hat, which had fallen when I had accelerated up the path. It seems he had seen me coming behind him as I passed the streetlight on the corner of West Street and First Avenue, and had hidden behind the tree, pulled his hat brim down, his coat collar up, picked up a broken limb and readied his flashlight as he awaited my arrival. He stepped out at just the right time and, as he said, he had "gotten me!"

44

Growing up, from early childhood to the false sophistication of high school life in the 1930's, was peppered with experimentation of all sorts. As they say, an idle mind makes an evil mind; we thought up all manner of pranks to play.

My peers and I would search the dumps that could be found behind most homes, bordered by banks or woods that partially hid their existence, for interesting finds such as unbroken light bulbs that no longer worked. Streetlight bulbs were highly prized. We would soak a string in kerosene, wrap it around the base of the bulb just above the metal portion, light it with a match and, as it burned off, break off the glass portion. This we filled with gunpowder and we then corked the top with a cork penetrated by a fuse. We now had a bomb of some potential that we would bring to Sabin's pasture and explode under resting rocks, watching from a safe distance as debris flew. We also tried making rockets of mailing tubes but met with little success, as most of our projects blew up like giant firecrackers after being lit. Metal tobacco cans made excellent bombs, although the danger multiplied with the flying bits of shrapnel they expended.

We made "Jolly Rogers," the flag of pirates with black background embossed with stark white skull and crossbones. Under cover of darkness and to the consternation of adults, we flew them from flagpoles around the city, twice flying our pennant from the flagpole in front of the State House, climbing the pole for a distance to secure the lanyard far above reach.

We used candle wax for graffiti on store windows, as it required scraping off and liberal applications of kerosene to remove. Other pranks we devised and used were universal at that time but one sticks in my mind as the epitome of all pranks. I was quite young when it was pulled off and only helped the instigators, much older than I, to perpetrate this unique and well thought out act. By sheer weight of numbers and with stealth supreme, a cow was led from Sabin's pasture and, by cajoling and brute strength walked up the staircases of the Administration Building of the Seminary and left on the third floor.

Cattle will walk up a stairway with some persuasion, but not down. The problem became a matter of logistics when trying to remove the animal. We roamed the outskirts as crews recruited from the city attacked the problem. Finally, late in the afternoon of the second day of attempts, and with judicious use of block and tackle, our undoubtedly hungry and thirsty cow, bellowing in protest, emerged from the building to be led back to the pasture, surrounded by men whose language was punctuated with epithets. Thereafter, the doors were locked early in the evening and when opened were guarded for a space of time by disgruntled janitorial staff.

45

In those long ago years of my growing up in Montpelier, many people impressed me greatly. One of them was "Hap" Deavitt. His rounded face was lit by a constant smile. Animated by a brisk swing of arms, he was encased in a nondescript jacket, threadbare and worn and ill fitting. Baggy pants held a belt cinched around his waist, ending in what we called "high water" style, showing either bare or sock-fitted feet thrust into either sandals or scuffed loafers. All of this was topped by what looked like a pile of rags on his balding head. Each year, Hap Deavitt was the true harbinger of spring.

When my first view of Hap was, I cannot say. I remember only that he came and left each year like clockwork. Spring, summer, and fall, he would be about the main streets of Montpelier. Because of his appearance, he was the object of ridicule among my peers. As the years passed, I learned through rumor some things about him that led me away from my childish thoughts to feelings of pity and compassion.

The story I was told was that he came from a once prominent Montpelier family. He had been educated in one of the Ivy League schools and had embarked on a career in law. For some reason, he had what we called in those days a "nervous breakdown" and was installed in our gracious State Hospital in Waterbury for a period of time. Sometime after his release, his mother died. He acquired a long roll of her hair, which he haphazardly fashioned into a kind of turban and pinned to his own locks. Since his hair was light brown in color and his mother's was a dark auburn streaked with white, the reddish highlights gleamed in the sunlight above his dull, sandy pate.

We assumed that because of his illness he would be unable to practice law, but through some arrangement with a local law office, he was employed as some sort of clerk during the time he was in Montpelier. Someone, although not confirmed, learned that he had a somewhat similar arrangement in New York City during the winter months. Whether any of this is true I can't attest to, although I can verify at least the sight of his hairpiece with my own eyes.

Very seldom would Hap say a word to any of us kids, but we would see him having conversations with the older folks on the corners of our city's intersection or seated on the steps of City Hall. Hap would stroll down the streets as knots of younger teens or adolescents snickered. Occasionally, derisive remarks would float from group to group. Hap would pace on as if not hearing the unwanted and unneeded salutations, all the while smiling that perpetual smile, nodding and talking to himself as if those annoyances did not exist. At times, some adult would speak to him and he would pause in his walk to talk briefly with them before pacing off again.

One early morning as I returned from fishing, I came face to face with Hap alone on the street. On impulse, as we were on a converging path, I called out cheerily, "Good morning" in a rather quavering voice, and Hap smiled as he passed me and answered in kind. Strangely, my fear of him flew off and a feeling of well being filled me. I thought, "There, that wasn't too bad, was it?" From that day, for some strange reason, I stopped being one of his detractors and felt sympathy toward him. He was still rather queer to my mind, but not the same as before when I had feared him, never sensing his harmlessness.

I never knew his first name, having never heard anyone use it. I knew only the name handed down by kids before me that "Hap" was for "happy". Deavitt was a more familiar name since one of Montpelier's more prominent blocks bore it in large letters on its façade.

As summer waned and the fall days sped to winter, a period of days would go by with no sightings of Hap and we would conclude that he had left us once again for his winter watch in the big city. Hap would be forgotten for that season, but would return as sure as the rising of the sun when winter had breathed its last the following year.

46

On Sunday, December 7th of 1941, Victor picked me up to help clean the barn on Trow Hill. We were just approaching the outskirts of Barre when the musical program we were listening to on the truck radio was interrupted for a news flash. The Japanese had just bombed Pearl Harbor in Hawaii and all was confusion. Details of the event were scarce and real anxiety was expressed in the commentator's voice.

Victor drove directly to his mother's house, which by that time was up by Spaulding High School off Washington Street. We rushed into the house where Victor's mother, sister, and brother-in-law were gathered around the radio in the living room. President Franklin Delano Roosevelt was just about to speak and all was hushed in the room in anticipation of his address. We were quite familiar with the sound of his voice, as he had given what came to be known as "Fireside Chats" often during the Depression to assure people that the economy would improve in time.

But on this cool and cloudy day, his voice seemed to quiver with what we supposed was rage, as his dulcet deep tones uttered the famous words, "December 7th, 1941, a day that will live forever in infamy." He told the American public that he had called a joint session of Congress to ask them to declare war on Japan. Later that evening, we heard him speak to Congress, which declared war, not only on Japan, but on Germany at the same time, following the lead of the Vermont Legislature which had met and declared war earlier in the day. America was now at war, and life as we knew it would change forever.

Immediate reaction to the realization of war might best be mirrored in my Uncle William's boastful statement that the war would only last six weeks before we conquered the Japanese. We were overconfident, actions proved otherwise. The loss of the Philippines was a shock that showed how ill prepared we were to wage war.

Enlistment of young men soon emptied the area of 18 to 25 year olds, and the draft took those at ages above. Even young men with families were not exempt from the service. Soon only men too young or too old to serve and those with physical defects were left.

In our neighborhood, the Magnes, Zonfrellos, Meladas, Seivwrights, Fitzgeralds, Babics, Comollis, Sykases, Garbacks, and others all had members in the service. The sight of many of them coming home for leave after basic training soon became quite common, and those leaving again on assignment, usually overseas, became a common occurrence. We missed them.

Although I have learned to be wary of causes because they usually are for one person or a select group's benefit, the rallying of all the people during World War II was an amazing experience in unity toward a common cause—the defeat of our enemies. With rare exception, all pitched in to uphold the war effort.

Rationing was handled with little complaint, for we knew these commodities would be in short supply. Sugar and flour were rationed, along with all meats and canned goods, bringing about the swift rise of black markets where those who could afford them could obtain scarce items. Along with this came the initiation of the term "hoarders", meaning those who stockpiled rationed items for their personal use. All who could not afford the items hated hoarders, and the government passed legislation to criminalize the act.

An official of the National Life Insurance Company, a much disliked, superior-acting man, was one of these. His imperious attitude alone justified the ill feelings of the common folks of the town. When his hoarding came to light, they greeted it with great joy.

It seems that the driver of an oil delivery truck, looking for the pipe to fill at the man's home, had discovered a large cache of sugar in bags stacked in the cellar. Enraged at finding the hoard, he overfilled the tank and allowed the oil to "accidentally" flow into the cellar, thus spoiling the sugar there. The oil company had to clean up the spill, but what could he say about his lost treasure? There was great joy shared over the incident when word got out, as it always would. Patriotic fervor was never expressed more fully.

Home Guards were organized with pride, and curfews were followed to the letter. Even airplane spotters, set up in small buildings on high points, were organized until late in the war when we realized no enemy was coming to attack us directly. Air raid warnings in the form of sirens mounted on tall buildings, such as the top of the Administration Building of Montpelier Seminary, were set up. Radio's first priority became the dissemination of war news, and newspapers and movie newsreels were devoted to reporting on the war. Everyone's thoughts in day-to-day life were constantly turned to the defense effort.

Victory Gardens soon sprouted from our former playing fields, until it was determined that the field we had used on the back side of the Administrative Building of the college had too much clay to be of any good, and we retained at least one field for our use. The main campus of the college was another site used, and it soon contained at least fifty gardens manned by people from all over town.

In the hysteria of the early war years, other measures were instituted. Either radio warning or blasts of the air raid siren usually signaled blackouts. They informed everyone to turn off all lights, including streetlights, pull the window shades, and maneuver by flashlight or candlelight in the home. After the initial excitement and thrill of blasting sirens and blackened nights several times in the belief that we were doing the right thing for the war effort, we tired of the experience and grumbled when next it happened.

Two things occurred to us that helped to dampen the enthusiasm of early days. First was the fact that, with no lights, we were sent to bed early, and second was the realization that it was only play-acting and that none of our enemies could reach us, particularly in the wilds of Vermont that had about as much strategic importance to the war as Death Valley. I also think upon reflection that the Victory Gardens and other activities, such as the kit bags made by women for distribution to the services, were part of a governmental program to encourage unity in the war effort, and had little bearing on the reality of the war. It was mostly to convince people that they were an integral part of it all.

Shortages did, of course, exist, especially in the early part of the war. Foods and other goods not essential to the war itself eventually began to appear in sufficient supply so that rationing slowly lagged off in time. The massive gearing-up of production of all commodities became, even with the Lend-Lease Program to a lot of the world, such that huge surpluses were experienced. With the coming of the middle forties, most of the rationed items, with the exception of meat, had been taken off the lists.

The Home Guard would periodically test the alarm mounted on the Ad Building as an exercise in preparedness. This became a great temptation to us, and once a week or so we would pull the lever and set the siren howling, usually late at night. At first, as we watched from a safe hiding place, the response was comical and frantic as the Home Guards in their white helmets would appear with shielded flashlights cutting the black night, cursing some unknown vandals. Soon, however, some genius among them came up with the ultimate solution to the problem. They put a lock on the alarm handle holding it down. They also put on patrols about Seminary Hill to catch the vandals.

We laid low for several weeks. Then, timing their patrols, we used bolt cutters on the lock and set the siren again. Once they used a huge lock, and in retaliation, after we had finally cut that off, we locked the handle in the up position and watched as they scurried around until they, too, cut the lock with bolt cutters.

Then they spoiled it all by parking a car by the entrance each night until morning and we tired of the game. So the Home Guard lost the battle but won the war, but only because we were becoming bored.

The first few weeks of gas rationing brought a diminishing of vehicular traffic. Downtown Montpelier had an abundance of parking spaces, and the bus to Barre became a packed affair. The noontime and after work homeward rush was a trickle of its former flow. Even Saturday night, which up to that time had been the busiest night of the week, the ultimate shopping time, was almost a vacuum.

This soon changed with the installation of the Army Specialized Training Program (ASTP) at Norwich University in Northfield. This was a program paid for by the services to train some of their soldiers for higher responsibility and rank. Admittance to the program was by examination, with the proviso that, if accepted, and on completion of the program, so many years were promised by you to be paid back in service. This depended on what your training was for.

From that time until war's end, crowds of these young men flooded the streets of downtown on weekends. Since most in the program were barely out of high school themselves, friction soon developed between the townies, and what we considered invaders on our turf. Montpelier Seminary had been taken over by Vermont College, and the greatest draw for males were the many girl students that now occupied the dormitories on the hill. Clashes became common on weekends as both groups vied for female companionship.

47

My freshman year brought one of the dreads we all faced—hazing. The upperclassmen at Montpelier High School usually lay in wait in the corridors to taunt all freshmen as they hurried to their first classes, stopping some to warn of dire things to come. Bud Sherman, Dean Slack, and I were pulled over one morning and told horror stories about what lay ahead for we three. We were told that Friday night we would be their victims, and we had better appear at Brother's Cafe on the corner of East State Street and Main at 7:30. All the rest of the week, we worried and talked among ourselves about what they might do to us. Among the list of horrors we had been informed of was the greasing of certain private parts with car grease. This we dreaded most, as we were still quite young and modest.

Friday night came all too soon, and we three joined the others at the site. Two or three in our class had big mouths and consequently were taken first out of our sight behind City Hall. When the gang of upperclassmen came to us, one of the group spoke up for us, I think it was Norm Laird, and said we weren't wise guys and had kept our mouths shut, so why not give us a head start and make a game of it. They finally agreed to give us fifty yards head start. We took off up East State Street, the whole bunch on our heels. They caught Slack as he ran across the campus of Vermont College, but Bud Sherman and I were still way ahead of them.

We rounded the corner of College and Sabin Streets and headed down Sabin. As we reached the corner, we heard part of the gang who had flanked us closing fast. The corner of Sabin Street had been used as a fill area for some years and extended some fifty feet from the street side to a precipitous drop of thirty feet to Sabin's Pasture. I yelled to Bud and we ran to the edge, looked back at the coming mob, and then jumped out over the edge. Luckily, we missed large blocks of granite and concrete from renewed roadwork and landed in soft dirt. Picking ourselves up, we raced into the darkness of the pasture.

Hidden by the dark, we stopped to see what they would do and to see if any had followed us. None had, and soon yells of disappointment came from the cliff edge with dire threats also directed at the dark night. Thus ended the affair for the two of us. Though some tried to catch me at a later date, I easily outran them and they finally begrudgingly gave up. We learned that the wise guy did get the grease, and a few others as well, but even Dean Slack who was caught got no real hazing.

48

After my freshman year of high school, I went to work for Mr. Cueto in his meat market during the summer months. And work it was. From seven in the morning until five in the afternoon, I swept the floor repeatedly, stocked shelves and cashiered. It made for a long day, especially working six days a week, and Saturday night till eight. One of my jobs was to cut up the cardboard boxes left over from stocking. I used a boning knife, a short, very sharp-bladed knife, to cut at the edges and then into squares for tying in bundles.

As I was cutting one day, I slipped on a piece of bone hidden in the sawdust beside the meat block, and stabbed myself in the knee. The knife's short length was buried just above the kneecap in the muscle and tendon there. It bled very little and it was close to closing time, so I thought little of it except for feeling a slight sting when I walked on it. When I arrived home, my wound was dressed. After eating, I hung around until bedtime, and then slept the night away.

When I awoke, my whole leg throbbed and my knee had swollen to twice its normal size. The family doctor was called, and after several hours he arrived to examine me. On looking at my wound, he concluded that I was bleeding internally beneath the kneecap. He called his nurse at the office. She soon arrived, bearing what looked to me like an enormous hypodermic syringe with a huge needle. She held my leg so that there was little movement while he pushed the needle into the side of my knee and drew the plunger back, filled with blood. After doing this several times, aspirating the fluid into a basin, he withdrew the needle and applied a fresh bandage, which he over-wrapped with a tight elastic bandage.

Twice a day for the next four days, he went through the same procedure. I lay on my back day and night in the same position with a pillow under my leg. On the fifth day, he concluded that the bleeding had stopped. With the admonition that I was to continue to stay in bed for one week more, he left me to my own devices. Despite the uncomfortable position and the boredom of having to stay in bed, the week passed and I was allowed up on crutches. My knee was still bound by the elastic bandage and had to remain straight, but I was allowed to lie on the day bed on the porch for another week. After this, the bandage was removed and

I was allowed to walk with crutches until just before my sophomore year started, for my knee would not bend without severe pain.

The first day of my sophomore year of high school at the Main Street School, as I worked my way up the stairs to my classroom, someone grabbed my leg and pulled. I screamed in pain and barely caught the stair railing as I collapsed, my crutches clattering down the stairs. It was Chuck Aguirre who had pulled my leg and who now stood in shock behind me. He had not meant to be malicious, but thought he was being playful. When I screamed and collapsed, he was all apologetic and concerned that he had hurt me.

As he helped me up the stairs, I noticed that, although my leg still hurt, I could now bend it again. He retrieved my crutches and I hobbled off to my classroom as he went to his. By the day's end, I was putting my full weight on the leg, and though it was still tender to do so, I was walking almost normally. In a few days, the pain lessened and the crutches were retired. I realized that Chuck, rather than being harmful, had in all probability done me a great favor by bending that knee and stretching those muscles and tendons. There's no telling how many weeks he saved me in therapy and pain by his sudden cure. Although I could not play football that fall, I could run again.

49

My first two years at Montpelier High School were under the guidance of Dr. John Huden, a principal with principles and a keen sense of humor. Dr. Huden was part Iroquois, a student of Indian ways, particularly of Vermont natives, and a much sought-after expert on the subject. He was a short, rather roly-poly man with a ready grin and sharp wit.

I remember three amusing incidents with clarity, the first being the day he caught Jim Seivwright and Raymond Alvarez fighting in the hallway. He stopped the fight and took them to the office. Later in the day, we learned that he had sent to the gym for two pairs of boxing gloves, made the two put them on, and held boxing lessons in his office. Every day for a week, Jim and Ray had to use their study hall time to go to the office for their boxing lessons. At the end of their week, we got to see what they had learned in front of the whole student body at assembly. There was no more fighting in the halls.

Frank Falacci had a habit of being late for his first class, and Dr. Huden, having noted this on the attendance records, decided Frank had been late too often. The Friday assembly gathered as it did each week, and when all notices had been read, Dr. Huden asked Frank to come up to the stage. With a speech dedicated to tardiness, he presented Frank with an alarm clock to help speed him to first class. A bright-faced, embarrassed Frank was never late again.

When a senior boy and junior girl were caught kissing by *The Thinker* statue in the hall, they were invited on stage the next Friday to demonstrate their technique. It made a profound impression on us all. The memory of John Huden will ever be a pleasant one of school days for me, especially since I knew him for such a short time.

In the spring of my sophomore year, on a stormy late May day darkened by rain and low clouds, flashes of lightning and windswept trees, Mrs. Huden had driven to the school to await the end of classes and give John a ride home. She had parked in front of the long walkway that led to the front door. She had just opened the car door to get out when a bolt of lightning struck one of the huge elms that grew along Main Street at the time. A large branch fell across the wires that lined that side of the street. The limb took the wires down across the car just as she stepped her foot out, and she and her children in the car were killed instantly. I happened to be in study hall at the time which was directly over the front door, and though none of us saw the instant of her death, we had all looked out when the limb crashed and the thunder rolled to see the car door half open and her foot on the ground. We knew immediately that something bad had happened. Our teacher had made us sit back down so we could not see more.

A commotion arose downstairs, and we later learned that Dr. Huden had tried to go to her, but had been restrained by several senior boys. They had to hold him on the floor for some time. He had seen the whole thing from his office window. He was in shock and hysterical over what he had witnessed, and was truly devastated. After a short time, police, firemen, and linemen appeared to take care of the wires and limb. The city doctor came, pronounced their demise, and took them away, as well as the car. We were all sent to the assembly hall, where we were talked to by several teachers, then held until the storm had passed, at which time we were allowed to go home.

Dr. Huden did not return for the rest of that year, and in the fall we had a new principal. We were told he was too grieved to continue at Montpelier High School, as was understandable. In later years I learned that he had gone back to UVM as a professor and I never saw him again. It was a great and profound tragedy in our lives. The halls of the high school were never the same from that time on. This man who gave so much of himself was repaid by fate in so stunning a manner.

50

Our high school was really a small building with high ceilinged, stark class-rooms and dark varnished wood floors. Two wide hallways ran the width of the building to the staircases on either end. Spotted here and there in this wide hall were large statues of various origins. A copy of Rodin's *The Thinker* stood along-side one of Pericles holding a spear in one hand, the other outstretched as if beg-ging for alms.

These near-naked forms were, on occasion, the recipients of graffiti. "Girls—do not touch" was once written next to the fig leaf covering Pericles' pri-vate area. On *The Thinker*'s forehead were the words, "Damn, somebody bring toilet paper", or on his thigh, "Here I sit brokenhearted, came to shit and only farted". Other antics included an unused condom draped in the beckoning hand of Pericles, and peanut butter smeared on the leg with the word "OOPS" above it. Mustaches of all description would appear from time to time, and I am sure we drove the janitors to distraction. Strangely, the statuary on the first floor seemed to remain unblemished, I suppose due to the fact that the main office was situ-ated there.

Study Hall, which everyone had, took up one period of our school day, usu-ally scheduled to each student at different times on different days. We were in what was called solid session, which meant we arrived at 7:30 a.m. and stayed until classes were over at 1:00 p.m., the only breaks being excused breaks for bathroom or disciplinary reasons. A short fifteen-minute break at 11:30 was given so that you could eat whatever you had brought for lunch. You had to stay in whatever room you were in at this time.

We had a farm boy in study hall who always slept through the period under the watchful eye of the monitor, who stared expectantly at him most of the time as he slept, supporting his head between his hands. More than once, having gone into deep REM time, his hands parted and his head struck the desk top with a resounding crash, waking him immediately. The monitor sympathized with his predicament of long early morning milking and chores, so let him sleep, but tried to catch him before his head hit.

In this particular study hall, we had an assortment of jokers who were con-stantly doing stupid things. One day, as my study hall came at the lunch break, I had brought a small jar of peanut butter and a small spatula to spread it, along with a half loaf of bread for my lunch. Someone threw a wad of spit paper at me and I retaliated by flicking some peanut butter on my spatula back at him. The next thing I knew, I was being challenged to flick peanut butter on the high ceiling of the hall. Naturally, with my very manhood in question, I had to meet the dare and proceeded to do so. We all watched in fascination as a glob stuck and then, ever so slowly, peeled off to drop back to the floor. I wiped this up, and as I was doing so, a senior by the name of Sergeant grabbed my jar and spatula and whipped back to his seat. He proceeded against my protests to flick peanut butter on the ceiling again and again. We watched the blobs drop slowly off it.

Just before the bell to end the period rang, he flipped a goodly glob onto the ceiling that refused to drop. The bell rang and he thrust the jar and spatula at me and left. I hurried to cover these in the bag I carried. I left for my next class and hoped I wouldn't be caught with the evidence. As soon as I could, I disposed of the bread and peanut butter and spent the rest of the day worrying. The next day all was serene, except for the pointing fingers of the jokers at the ceiling where the peanut butter glob reposed. Curiosity got the best of the bunch and bets were made as to when it would either come down or be discovered by the school authorities. On the day of graduation from good old MHS, we noted that no one had won their bet, as the peanut butter had become a permanent decoration on the ceiling of study hall.

51

At the age of 16, I was asked to join Clan Gordon #12 of the Royal Order of Scottish Clans, a fraternal organization based in Barre. Several boys my age were to join together, some from Montpelier, but most from Barre. Jim Seivwright, my cousin William and I were driven over to the clan hall on the night of our investiture to meet all the others in an anteroom just off the main hall. After waiting an eternal half hour, we were escorted into the main hall by the clan tanner, a sort of secretary of the organization.

To my surprise and dismay, as they lined us up I was put at the head of the line. As we walked in following the tanner, I was placed in a chair facing the clan officers, alone in front of the others. I had no idea why I was being singled out to be in this position and it made me extremely nervous. We went through fraternal instruction and, upon taking an oath of allegiance, were declared clan members in good standing.

Then the Chief of the clan asked me to stand alone. He declared that, since my grandparents were from Huntley, Aberdeenshire, I was a true Gordon Clansman, which met with applause. Embarrassed and red-faced, I still did not know the significance of all these doings.

After the ceremony, when things had quieted down for the social hour, George Seivwright approached me and asked how I felt about all the attention. I told him I was totally bewildered about it all. He then explained some of my ancestry. Up until that time, no one had spoken of it, although I knew both Mother and Father were Scots. I had asked questions about it and received no satisfactory explanations. I learned that Huntley was the seat of Clan Gordon and that Websters were born under the protection of the Gordons. It was unusual within Clan Gordon #12 to have a blood tie to the Gordons, for most members were from other ancestral clans. It had been a coincidence more than anything else, but I wish I had been prepared.

So as a newly proud Gordon, I played a game of pool and promptly tore the table felt. Kind of evened the evening out.

At the age of sixteen, I also got talked into joining the State Guard. Since the National Guard had been called up and sent to the South Pacific to fight the war, it left a void to be filled by a state militia. The legislature had voted a State Guard to be filled by those men left from enlistment in the regular service or over age for the draft. They had found that they could not fill their quota, and had lowered the age of enlistment in the guard to sixteen in desperation. Several of my friends had joined, and peer pressure prevailed until I submitted as well. We were all assigned to the company lodged at the Barre Street Armory.

A few older officers and non-coms introduced us to the manual of arms at training one night a week. My mother had also joined as a secretary in the Commander's office. The Company Commander was Captain Laurence Gauthier, and Battalion Commanders were Majors Keith Murray and Dr. Edmunds, DDS. Dr. Edmunds was my dentist, a hard-drinking man whose conduct at encampments was legendary. Keith Murray had been wounded in the war, sent back home to recover, discharged, and then commissioned in the State Guard. He was a really good officer with a sense of humor, well thought of by all.

Our encampments were held at the Tunbridge Fairgrounds on weekends, plus a weeklong one each summer. One weekend a month, we either went on encampment or stayed from Friday night to Sunday evening at the Armory. We were paid the same as regular service people, by rank and length of service. We also were allowed to use the basketball court when it was not in use by the Guard and, with supervision, were allowed to use the shooting gallery in the basement.

On the first encampment at Tunbridge, we held guard duty, riot training, shooting on range, and general manual of arms training. Military discipline was paramount. We held a grand review on the Saturday before we left, with all units in the state marching around the trotting track. It was a slight magnification of Boy Scout training, only at adult level.

The nights, after retreat was sounded and before final taps, were our own within the limits of the fairgrounds. This left us time to visit with other units and to learn the fine art of drinking, since this was the main entertainment of the older officers and men. I had my first beer, which I promptly threw up. That completed my course in a hurry. I did, however, observe the various reactions of others, such as the legendary Dr. Edmunds who slurped a raw egg before chug-a-lugging his beer. I watched a full dozen eggs slide down his throat in one evening and, to my mind, he was not very impaired by the exercise. In fact, in the morning after that Saturday night, he performed in an absolutely sober manner, his faculties plenty sharp.

Others who I am sure imbibed much less were haggard, gray faced, and in obvious pain from monstrous hangovers. I think that is when I had an inkling begin to penetrate my brain, and I started to understand that some could and some could not hold their liquor. I realized that I was of the latter, despite what I might have inherited for genes from my father. Though I did drink some in later days, it was always with that thought in the back of my mind. Despite having to bear the stigma of my father's behavior, and being constantly reminded of it by my mother with the words, "You're just like your father", I never developed a taste for brew and only tolerated liquor when being sociable.

In the spring of my junior year, a fire destroyed the old arsenal on College Street. Left over from Civil War days, the brick edifices blazed furiously as their wooden insides flamed, becoming an inferno. The only two buildings not destroyed were the caretaker's house and, luckily, the old powder house, where all the ammunition was stored. All that day and through the next night we stood our posts, blocking all traffic on both ends of College Street and allowing only people who lived in houses adjacent to the compound to pass, as curiosity seekers and local residents came to gaze at the destruction.

We were relieved for only an eight-hour period, and then were back at guard again for another twenty-four hour stretch. This time, we were allowed eight hours of sleep sandwiched between eight hours of full duty in shifts. This went on for a full week, until all ammunition and other equipment was trucked out of the compound. Missing school was a happy prospect, but sleeping on cots set up in squad tents got to be a little hairy, as it rained for several days toward the end of our week on duty. We were all soaked to the skin from splashing around the area and, even with rain gear, managed to stay that way. It was my first taste of what my service days would become and I already hated the discomfort of it.

Mother and Larry had developed a romantic interest between them while together in the Guard and it was only a matter of time before, upon the finalization of his divorce from his wife, they were married in a civil ceremony and I had been presented with a stepfather.

52

In the late 1930's and early 40's, I had acquired a small, battered, temperamental radio that refused to hold stations tuned in from any distance. Although this presented a definite problem, I turned it on every night while getting ready for bed. Since I slept in the same room as my brother Donald, I adjusted the volume barely loud enough to hear beside my bed in line with my pillow.

At nine o'clock, my favorite program came on the air from a New York station—WNEW, as I remember—with the announcement, "From the ballroom atop the Hotel Astoria in the center of downtown New York." It was *Make Believe Ballroom Time* with a different big band featured each night.

After much delicate tuning, I would lay back with my head on the pillow, the radio at my bedside within six inches of my ear, and listen to the melodious sounds of Glenn Miller, Tommy Dorsey and brother Jimmy, Tony Pastor, Count Bassie, Duke Ellington, Charley Barnett, Louis Armstrong, Les Brown with his Band of Renown, Spike Jones, Benny Goodman, Guy Lombardo, Woody Herman, Artie Shaw, Swing and Sway with Sammy Kaye, and others, for a full hour.

Saturday nights were the time for *The Hit Parade*, a melodious mélange of the top tunes of the day where new songs often appeared for the first time. On both shows, the Big Band sounds came through to us, and we were introduced to new performers such as The Inkspots, the Everly Brothers, Frank Sinatra, The Andrews Sisters, Helen Morgan, The Maguires, Connie Francis, and others, as well as old-time favorites Bing Crosby, Kate Smith, Gene Krupa, Tex Beneki, Bunny Barrigan and Harry James.

Most music after 1941 had to do with the war and ranged from *Boogie Woogie Bugle Boy, You're in the Army Now*, and other propaganda tunes to *White Cliffs of Dover, A Nightingale Sang on Barclay Square, Roll out the Barrel, Love Letters*, and others that were sentimental or nostalgic. The Andrews Sisters had a big hit in a tune called *Don't Sit Under the Apple Tree*, a ditty that expressed the feelings of the men who had left home and country with pangs of jealousy.

The men who were not accepted into the service for physical reasons were classified as 4-F, a designation which became a sort of stigma for those left behind, regardless of their personal desire to be with their friends. The term 4-F became almost a shameful thing, especially as more families sported the Gold Star insignia in the windows of their homes. Though faultless, they were disparaged in conversations and thought to be less "manly" than those who went to fight the war. This became the only pool of men left, except for those whose situation in life made them declared essential to the home front. Human nature being what it is, this caused a lot of the women left alone to take advantage of their presence. As a result, the words "Don't sit under the apple tree with anyone else but me" struck a chord that resounded among those in the service. Never think for a moment that these were usual circumstances, as most wives and girlfriends stayed extremely loyal to those away and were equally faithful in their patriotic life, but the dread of the sometimes very real "Dear John" letter still niggled the minds of many.

Most of the Big Bands were broken up by the call to service, although with replacements managed to keep going. Difficulties rose mainly concerning transportation, but somehow they managed to make the rounds all over the country to small towns as well as large cities, either by rail or bus, to play at local dance halls. We were fortunate indeed to see several of these bands perform in at least two places in Vermont, the Pavilion in Newport and the Mallets Bay Pavilion in Colchester. These were the only dance halls large enough to hold the huge crowd needed to pay for the band's performance. Both pavilions were also used for roller-skating and had been built as large, single-floored buildings.

Although called a dance, the huge crowd of several hundreds of wall-to-wall people were packed in so tightly that anything other than foot movement was impossible, so we stood tightly wedged and listened the entire evening in rapt attention to the musicians, talking for days after of the "dance." I attended when several bands played in these places, among them Glenn Miller, Tommy and Jimmy Dorsey, Louis Satchmo Armstrong and Les Brown. I always felt I was lucky to see and hear Glenn Miller, because he went into the service shortly after and was killed. Going to the dances was an experience I've always had fond memories of, and today can still feel and hear the music as though it were only a yesterday away.

Joe's Pond had a small dance hall that we frequented when we could cop a ride. Small local bands played there and produced good music of the day. The dances were held from Memorial Day through the summer, ending on Labor Day. The crowds were usually very good and, aside from the occasional drunk who became obnoxious, everyone had a good time. Kate's Barn in Calais, Silverdome in Brookfield, Duxbury Grange Hall, and East Montpelier Town Hall held combinations of popular and square dancing that I attended at times. Sunset

Pavilion in the hills above Barre had a rough-edged reputation for drunken fighting, so I went with trepidation only a few times. Although I attended all these in my high school days infrequently, I went more often after I got out of the service.

In Montpelier, other than an occasional school or church dance at Bethany Church basement and the movies, there was little in the form of entertainment for high school aged students. The main hangout downtown, other than the bank corner at State and Main Streets, was an establishment known as Barquin's, a small ice cream parlor with about eight booths and a soda fountain. The most popular beverage served was Coca-Cola, the most ordered drink cherry cokes, and the most popular dessert hot fudge sundaes, only partaken of by those whose fortunes had taken an upward swing.

Rules were firmly established as to behavior, and penalties were applied with vigor. The absolute worst punishment was expulsion for various lengths of time. Anyone forced to leave was usually expelled for two weeks, and was shattered by the experience. Not to be allowed to hang out with your peers was devastating. You could usually tell who the expelled were by observing who crowded the sidewalk in front of Barquin's, as they hung as close as they dared.

Mr. and Mrs. Barquin must have had the patience of Job. Aside from an occasional request to not block the doorway, they totally ignored the crush outside. When your time was up, you were again welcomed in, with the admonition to behave yourself, and all was wonderful again. How they put up with us, I'll never know.

All these places were where we came to see and be seen. What you wore made all the difference. In the forties, the most popular shoe was the saddle shoe. Made in the form of the white buck shoe, they had a strip of leather that came from the instep to the laces in either black or brown color. Everyone wore this shoe, or the fairly new loafer with a penny stuck in the band above the instep, whenever they were not wearing the versatile sneaker. Pants in a variety of colors were worn with a white shirt and a tennis sweater over it. The coat of choice was full length, tan camel hair. I remember my first camel hair coat, for which I had yearned for a long time. I always felt sharp whenever I wore it, and I wore it until the nap was gone. With great reluctance, I finally had to replace it. Girls wore much the same clothing, except for skirts that came below the knee and bobby sox, which were the new rage of the day. In my junior year, I bought my first pair of white bucks that were just becoming popular, and wore them most of my life thereafter.

53

In the early 1940's, Kate Colombo, who owned the house we lived in, decided to sell it, so we moved to Summit Street, the street at the head of Edwards Street that paralleled Foster. It was a short move and we remained in our old neighborhood. Our new house was owned by George Seivwright and stood adjacent to his. Although a smaller house, we all managed to fit in, albeit tightly. Nonie had married and moved out, and everyone had to double up for bedroom space—even the upstairs hall alcove was used as a bedroom. There was only one bathroom upstairs, but we were used to that. A large kitchen, dining room, living room, and foyer made up the rest of the house.

It had a large, spacious cellar that had an enclosed shower in one corner. Hot water was supplied through a coal-fired water heater. Building the small coal fire before taking a shower took some planning, because it took about an hour to heat enough water to ensure not freezing from a rush of cold water at shower's end. There were arguments sometimes when someone took advantage of your fire to slip in before you could, but other than that, we got along well.

Donald and I were still sleeping in the small bunk beds we had used for years and, although having un-bunked them. I was growing taller. My feet were always braced against the footboard, my head brushing the headboard. I had learned to curl my body onto the side to avoid this, but often during the night awoke from pressure on my feet or pain on my head as I stretched unconsciously. I also realized that, having looked up to the adults in the family for so long, I was now looking down on all of them, even my tall aunt Buddy. I had developed a voracious appetite and was aware that I now had shoulders and a chest, as well as bigger thighs and calves. I became increasingly conscious of my strength when objects I had struggled with in the past became easy to move.

I worked a large garden and mowed the lawn, even the steep banks, with a regular push lawnmower. Although I no longer had to handle wood for heat, due to our oil furnace, I had other chores to attend to. I had, of course, also become aware of girls and had begun to date them, thus changing my outlook on my daily life.

My Grandmother Ewen still ruled the family with an iron hand, and Edith was still the enforcer of her edicts. Up to that time, I had to toe the mark as everyone else did. One Friday evening as I prepared to go on a date, Edith met me at the front door with crossed arms guarding the door. I was told that because of some real or imagined slight of my duties, I was not allowed out that night. Suddenly my temper rose in my chest. I answered quite calmly that she had better step away from the door or I would move her out of my way. A shocked expression sprang onto her face. With a widening of her eyes, she stared back at my expression and towering height and moved aside.

As I opened the door to step out, she snapped, "The door will be locked to you." I stopped, turned and faced her, and said, "If the door is locked on my return, I'll break it down." I then left the house and proceeded off on my date. It was with some apprehension and a lot of determination that I returned home, to find the door unlocked. I went to bed, and upon arising in the morning was greeted normally. Nothing more was said to me about the incident, although I noticed a definite difference in the way they looked and talked to me. Life seemed to proceed without further incident and a sort of balance was established. I still deferred to them around the house, but they left me alone to my chores as I saw fit and never tried to stop me going out again.

54

School, sports, and girls kept me busy during my high school, school being boring, sports exciting, and girls more so. I played baseball, football, and briefly went out for track, spliced in among my hunting and fishing. I also participated in plays and chorus, as well as student council.

School was a bore. The problem was many-faceted, in that most of my teachers at that time were either older and bored themselves, or younger and not taught very well. Those teachers that could inspire seemed to all be in the service or working in Connecticut where the big money was. Pratt and Whitney aircraft was booming with the war effort and paying unheard of wages in the 1940's, so anyone with ambition went to work there. Vermonters were welcomed with open arms, with the reputation for working full weeks, including overtime, without sick leave or other excuses for management to contend with. At any rate, I did not think very highly of the teachers I had, with only two exceptions in four years.

We had just acquired the services of a young teacher who, if you didn't know her, you would assume to be another student. She was sadly unlearned in her topic area of American History. I'm sure she read one chapter ahead of the class, and taught badly. On the day of our first class on the Revolutionary War, she announced that the beginning of the war was in 1776. Not being shy, I spoke up and corrected her, quoting the date of Concord and Lexington in April of 1775. I was immediately sent to the office to wait upon the good graces of Dr. Chastney to be reprimanded.

Dr. Chastney, on my being announced by his secretary, sighed and asked what I was there for this time. I explained the circumstances as he listened, shaking his head slowly. He then said that, although I was correct, I should not have embarrassed the teacher in front of the whole class. After spending a pleasant period of time with the good doctor, I went on to my next class with his admonition to try to be a little more tactful from then on. I tried very hard to ignore her future errors. Although I never handed in any homework that year, I passed all exams with the highest marks in all her classes. Most of my knowledge I had previously learned by reading on my own.

She was an equally poor disciplinarian. As the year progressed, the students took the upper hand. Bob Kynock was one of those who had taken her measure and found it wanting. He established a cocky attitude with her and took advantage of it. One day, just as class was about to begin, he went to his usual seat to find someone in it. Arguing with the seated student, he was told by her to find another seat. He then started to argue with her about the seating. Suddenly there was a deep-toned voice heard from the back of the class that said, "Why don't you come up and sit with me?" All eyes went to the back of the room where the Superintendent of Schools, Mr. McClelland, sat. With a slight hesitation and evident reluctance, Bob walked to the back and sat in the seat Mr. McClelland indicated and class started. Bob left at the end of class accompanied by Mr. McClelland, turning toward the office and his fate. If Mr. McClelland was looking for teaching and discipline from our teacher, he got direct insight into the lack of it in our class that day. Bob Kynock, from that day on, heard the words, "Why don't you come up here and sit with me!" quite often from us all.

Despite not doing any homework, I had the only A+ in the finals at year's end, much to the chagrin of that particular teacher who, I am sure, would have liked to flunk me. I was given a B+ because of my lack of homework for the year. It was much the same in most of my classes. Although I would do other people's homework in study hall for them, I seldom did my own. I was being stupid and stubborn I now know, and I hurt only myself by doing it.

One day, I was late for English class where we were studying Shakespeare. After taking my seat, I was scolded for being late. Since we were studying *MacBeth*, I was told to read MacBeth's soliloquy out loud as a kind of punishment. Instead, I recited the entire thing from memory, as she looked at me with amazement and disappointment that her ploy had backfired. She was so enraged that she sent me to the office upon completion of my recitation. Once again, I had made a teacher look bad in front of class. Dr. Chastney went through his head-shaking routine and admonitions, and then we chatted as usual.

Mr. Glenn Aiken was one of the few teachers I had who could teach and inspire, as all good teachers should. He also had a sense of dry Vermont humor that complemented his demeanor. Since we had a small science class of only ten students, informality was accepted so that everyone could partake in discussion at will. Experiments could be set up rapidly and everyone could participate in the group at once.

One day, Glenn was late getting to class. We knew we had about fifteen minutes before he would arrive while he was tied up with another class. This gave us the opportunity to wire some of the instruments to be used in that day's class and attach them to a Leyden jar so that, if picked up, they would shock whoever handled them. Glenn arrived, and after a little discussion, proceeded to set up the experiment, reaching for our wired parts. He was talking as he picked up the first part with his left hand and continued on as nothing happened. He then requested that Bob Kynoch help him. When Bob touched the first of his parts, blue flame erupted. Bob howled, dropping the part. Our trick had clearly backfired.

With a grin on his face, Glenn explained that his left hand, slightly crippled by polio as a child, did not sweat, and therefore could not conduct electrical impulses without the presence of water to conduct it through the hand. Bob thought our wiring faulty and assumed that it wouldn't affect him either. We all learned two valuable lessons in class that day. One was the demonstration of electric conductivity. The other was not to mess with Glenn in class, for he clearly had read our trick by our actions and expressions before he had extended that left hand.

I wrote two papers for his class that earned me A+'s, not only in physics, but also in English class, where I used them both for term papers. One was on the aerodynamics of flight, in which I explained not only the principles, but also by diagram and writing predicted the flying wing, as I called it. Glenn was a Navy officer. He sent that paper to the Navy, who tried to recruit me into the Naval Air Training Program at Norwich University. Mother would not sign the papers, even after they talked to her, because she believed that college was not necessary.

The second paper was on atomic principle and this too aroused much interest from the Navy, and much bewilderment from my English teacher, who could not understand it. She therefore marked not on content but on correctness of grammar and English usage only. Again, Mother prevailed in preventing me to enter the field, believing that the space program and flying saucers were in the hoax category together. I am forever grateful to Glenn Aiken for sparking my interests in science and technology.

55

My freshman year on the football team we won all our games. I was halfback on a single wing team and really enjoyed running the ball and scoring touchdowns. Then came the disaster of my not being able to play my sophomore year due to the injury at Cueto's Market the previous summer. Our coach those two years was Danny Alvino, one of the "seven blocks of granite" in college ball when Fordham was a football power. Gray Coane, our previous coach, had also been on that team, along with Vince Lombardi, future coach of the Green Bay Packers. Gray Coane had gone into the service just prior to my freshman year and had convinced Danny Alvino to coach in his stead. He stayed only two years before going on to coach in college, after we had won the state championship in the unbeaten season of my sophomore year. Incidentally, Gray Coane married Vince Lombardi's widow in a later year.

In my junior year, we had a new coach. Coach Harvey did not have much going for him except that he was a nice older guy. He was very soft spoken and quiet talking, with very little control of the team. His discipline was lax, and often he wouldn't even show up at practice, leaving us to our own devices. He was a nice guy, but as Leo 'The Lip' Durocher, the famous Brooklyn Dodgers manager said, "Nice guys finish last." The amazing thing is that we won more than we lost, but only because our competition was worse.

The first day of practice we had rush spurts to see how fast we were. I was the fastest. Since I had played halfback as a freshman, I figured I would go to the backfield again. Instead, Coach Harvey lined us up and chose me as a tackle because I was tall. So I played tackle for two years, and the backs struggled to pass the scrimmage line with their slow steps. Dean Slack and I teamed up as tackles and did a serviceable job at it, but my heart was never in it like it would have if I'd been running the ball. I later played halfback in the service on an unbeaten team.

I remember watching Frank Falacci, the center, standing over the ball, blowing his nose with his fingers, then bending over and centering the ball back. That was one time I was glad I wasn't in the backfield. Another time we were playing a game at the old Burlington field on a rain-driven day, the field a clay quagmire. There was a pile-up in the center of the line, and the ball squirted upward and out along the line. It came right to me and I started to run on a clear muddy field to the goal line. I had gone about ten yards, was clear with the goal in site, when I was hit from the side by my teammate Pete Sykas in a perfect tackle, and down I went. We lost the game 7-0, thanks to Pete's superb tackle.

We played two teams that were so bad that we took pity on them. St. Albans had a poor team my senior year. The first play from scrimmage, Slack and I hit the opposing tackle hard, Slack going low as I went high. There was a loud snap and the tackle screamed in pain. We had broken his left leg. The rest of the game, we played shoulder to shoulder and just stood our ground. It was the longest game I remember playing in my life.

Another team that was very weak was Lyndon, in a game played late in the season. When the score reached 42-0, we started running out of backfield subs and substituted line members to slow us down. It did not work, as they too scored, and only time stopped the slaughter. At first it felt good to score at will, but after a while we began to feel bad for the opposing team, and left with a bad taste for the day. Not that this sort of thing happened every Saturday. We lost to Spaulding, Rutland and Burlington in both my junior and senior years, and to Mt. St. Joseph in my junior year.

Baseball we played rather loosely with little or no coaching. We had fun, but our losses were a common occurrence in a season of ups and downs. Track was even worse than baseball, both in coaching and ability, as we were the first school other than Burlington (who had a coach and experience) to field even an incomplete team. No other schools had track, so we competed individually against each other for the season, holding only two meets with Burlington. We did not offer much competition for them. There were no sports teams for girls at Montpelier High School while I attended.

All transportation for sporting events was by cars driven by interested and loyal high school sports fans. We had no public buses furnished by the school system. Sometimes away games had to be delayed until all of our teams could arrive at their destinations, since some would inevitably lose their way or have car trouble.

One incident, not sports related but coach related, happened in study hall in my sophomore year. Danny Alvino was substituting as study hall proctor that day. Frank Falacci was sitting at the desk in front of me, conducting a running conversation with Mahlon Garback, who sat to his right in the next row of desks. Coach Alvino had already singled Frank out and told him to be quiet. Study halls were run like libraries, in that no talking was the rule. I had my head down studying a part for a play I was in and was concentrating on memorizing my part.

As sudden as a bolt of lightning, an arm shot across the upper part of my vision. As I jerked back in surprise, Coach Alvino grabbed Frank by the collar of his shirt and heaved him up over his lift-top desk. As Frank rose and was pulled forward, the top went with him, breaking off as the hinges reached their limit. When Frank reached the apex of his ride, the desktop tore off and clattered onto the floor. Frank kept going over the desk and onto the floor in front of it, then up the aisle as Coach Alvino, his grip never varying, pulled him all the way, his feet dragging along the door and out to the hallway. Coach then slammed Frank up against the far wall with a fist brandished in Frank's face, told him that he had warned him to shut up and would now knock his G. D. head off. All this was said in a fury of rage. Frank's pasty white face could be seen over Coach's shoulder as he protested to the coach.

All of us had jammed the doorway following Coach and Frank on their exhilarating journey to the hallway. One senior, Ed Sawyer, ran out and calmed Alvino down by low talk, and Frank was released to quickly duck around him and race down the hall and staircase, to where we knew not. Nor did we ever learn the aftermath of this violent incident. We did, however, note that Coach Alvino did not have study hall again, and that Frank remained quiet as a church mouse when there.

56

In the fall of my senior year, Mother and Larry were married in a civil ceremony on October 24, and big changes were made in my life. Larry purchased the Somers house at 25 Ridge Street and we moved into the upstairs apartment, inadvertently precipitating another clash with a teacher of mine.

I was in the play *Romeo and Juliet*, under the direction of Miss Alice Edwards, our drama teacher. Larry never had much patience, and when he had made a decision to do something at a particular time, that was it. Larry decided that we would move in on a Friday night. I had a dress rehearsal that same evening. I told him I had to be there, since I had the part of Paris, one of the leading roles. Naturally, I was told I would have to skip rehearsal to make the move, so I did. After two quick trips moving small items and clothing, he decided to finish the next day. As it was only 6:30 and rehearsal was scheduled for six o'clock, I raced to the Union School auditorium, figuring that, although late, I could still participate.

I opened the door to the hall and was greeted by the most vituperative yelling and screaming I had ever heard, punctuated with swearing. "Son of a bitch!" and "Bastard!" and more was coming from Miss Edwards, standing center stage. I stopped, stunned by this tirade and ingested the words. With my temper rising, I replied loudly in kind, with such sobriquets as "bitch" thrown in. Evidently, no one had ever called her that before, and she immediately seemed to calm, leaving the stage to approach me. We went out into the hall where she reproached me for my outburst and I, in turn, reproached her for hers.

After a short period of discussion, we agreed on a truce and returned to the auditorium to calmly play our parts of actor and director, to the amazement of the cast and stagehands. Dress rehearsal went well. She and I never spoke of the incident again, although many of the cast spoke of it with some awe for a while. The play was a huge success, winning much acclaim for Miss Edwards, who left after my senior year for Broadway. I have often wondered what might have happened had Dr. Chastney heard our little tiff, and have concluded that I would probably have been expelled and Miss Alice Edwards most likely would have been fired.

Not long after this incident, Larry and I had words. It seemed that on a night when I was supposed to be home by eleven o'clock, I didn't quite make it there until 11:15. I admitted that I didn't make it home by the time I was supposed to, and apologized for being late. That encouraged him to pursue the subject *ad nauseum*. Although I had by then learned to control my temper somewhat, it still took hold of me on occasion with blinding fury, and I could feel it coming on as he berated me. Then he made a big mistake and tried to grab my arm as I headed for my bedroom. That did it. Although I managed not to strike out, I did pick him up by the shirtfront and bounce him off the wall. Real fear showed in his eyes and face as I held him at arms length and choked out, "Don't ever lay a hand on me!" I then released him, fighting all the time for control of my temper. I told him I would obey his wishes as closely as possible, but he was never to touch me again. We talked for a while and mutually agreed to those terms, which I did abide by in good faith from that time on. I came to respect him as a person and I believe he did the same with me.

57

As far as romance went, it was a strange, thrilling time in my life. My biggest problem with girls was trying to keep my relationships from becoming serious. I guess what I was, besides innocent, was just plain scared. When things got too warm, I just walked away. The amazing thing is that the girls didn't seem to be hurt by my inaction or offended by my refusals. Two things occur to me—I never dated a girl in my class in school and I only broke up with one girl in my life. I know it's not an enviable record, but I never had an angry girl bad-mouthing me or ignoring me in later life. I had fun and they seemed to as well, even the disappointed ones.

Marie Bisson was one girl for whom I never had romantic notions. As a matter of fact, she was really a girl friend. I used to go to her house several evenings a month to listen to her great record collection. Marie was the daughter of Dr. Bisson who lived in a large house on Center Street that had a rumpus room, as we called it, in the cellar. The rumpus room was pine-paneled and furnished with comfortable furniture. On one end of the room was a sort of built-in bed or sofa with massive pillows, lit by side lighting. Beside this on one wall was installed a record player with stereo speakers, which were unheard of at the time, and a huge bank of records, all popular music.

Marie went to St. Michael's Catholic High School. We would meet at Barquin's after school for the usual cherry cokes and discussion of the day. We remained friends until I went into the service and she went off to college. Then we saw each other less frequently. Our lives just seemed to drift apart, although I would hear from her through her girl friends who remained in the Montpelier area.

Frank Sinatra was just becoming popular and Marie had every record he had ever made. We would listen for hours to the melodious crooning of Frank, broken occasionally by the latest Bing Crosby, Vic Damone, Perry Como, or others that flashed onto the charts. We listened on Saturday nights to hear the new hits on *Hit Parade*, the most popular radio show for teens. If a record made the *Hit Parade*, record sales would follow and popularity was ensured, even to the point of nominations to the Golden Record awards.

58

High School passed surprisingly fast, and before I realized it, graduation was upon us. It was held in Montpelier City Hall on a Friday June night, a sultry evening brought on by a hot humid spell. In our black robes, we stood on Main Street in the hot sun for what seemed like hours before filing into the hall. Long boring speeches preceded our actual ceremony. Although all the others in my class had received their Silver M's and other academic awards at a previous ceremony at the school, I was given mine at graduation because of a mix-up in the school records. The Silver M was awarded to students who had maintained a B average or better.

I had taken a Commercial Course my first two years of school and, having completed all the required courses with the exception of English, had elected to change to a College Prep course my junior and senior years. This confused the records, since normally one stayed with whatever course one started. Upon further examination of my records after the awards ceremony, it had been discovered that, despite my lack of effort, I had indeed earned a B average throughout both courses. This entitled me to the Silver M and other honors, which they reluctantly had to bestow on me. So they had to single me out for this, as well as give me my diploma at graduation. Embarrassing to both parties!

After graduation, initial notice of the draft board was sent to us. This meant we had to register at the Post Office for the draft although we were not of age yet to be drafted. Most of us not already registered with a college thought about going into the service and getting it over with. Dean Slack, Pit Normandeau, and I were three that decided to join up, as it had guarantees of certain privileges if you joined ahead of the draft. I went on to boot camp at Camp Kilmer in New Jersey, and then to the worst camp in the country, the tarpaper shacks of Fort McClellan. After a two-month leave at home, I shipped out to Japan and was assigned to the 11th airborne, I Company, Camp Schimmelfennig in Sendai, Japan, a newly formed base named after a Civil War veteran.

Mother, at some point in the late 1930's, had left the employ of the telephone company to join a new agency of the state government called Unemployment Compensation, which was partially funded by the Federal Government under the NRA. A brilliant man who had written a book on Vermont's wildflowers that drew national attention headed this agency. Somewhere in the span of that time, Mother had become his secretary, remaining in that position until his rise to the position of Governor of the State of Vermont. For some reason known only to Mother, she refused to follow him as his secretary in that position but remained on a friendly basis with him. This, of course, was George Aiken, who went on from his Governorship to become one of the leading senators in Congress as the years progressed.

George still maintained connections with Montpelier. His daughter, Dot, married Harry Morse of the large Morse farm in East Montpelier, so George visited on those weekends he could. One of those times, Mother met him on the street and asked him if he would check up on me, as she had received no word from me since I had left from my leave. The circumstances I had been through in my transport to Japan had not been conducive to writing until I was finally settled in my second barracks. That, combined with the obvious slowness of the Army Post Office in getting the mail back to the states, had delayed letters I had written since. She had not heard from me for a couple of months. Senator Aiken replied that he would look into it and Mother, being satisfied in this, went on her merry way, not knowing what a can of worms she had inadvertently opened.

Senator Aiken, on arrival in Washington, found several new problems demanding his immediate attention. He did meet with Senator Austin, then head of the U.S. Delegation to the United Nations, and asked him if he would follow up on my mother's problem. Senator Austin contacted the Secretary of Defense, who in turn sent the request on to the Commander of the Far East Command, General MacArthur, who in turn sent inquiry down his chain of command to 11th Airborne Headquarters. General Swing then reacted by sending a Brigadier General and a Colonel from Headquarters to our Regimental Commander for instant action. Not being aware of this scenario, I was called into the Colonel's office and read the riot act in no uncertain terms. Those terms were that I sit right there and write a letter to Mother which would be sent by courier to MacArthur's headquarters, thence on down to her with all the proper endorsements attached. Then, being further blasted, I was to write a letter each week under the eyes of one of the 11th airborne headquarters' colonels until they were satisfied I was complying with those orders. Although I was accorded some degree of fame, or infamy, depending on direct or indirect contact, I was grateful when it was decided I had followed orders and could be left to my own devices.

59

My enlistment had been for a three-year period, but due to cutbacks in defense funding between World War II and the Korean War, I along with most of my comrades in arms was sent home for discharge after only a little more than one year's service. We were still Uncle Sam's property for those months until our original enlistment passed and we were eligible for time in active reserve.

Having made it home without further incident, I now had to make only the slight adjustment back to civilian life; that is, in addition to having to go back to sharing a room with my brother. I also found little in the way of my possessions still there. My mother had discarded all my treasures through the years, as she said, in an effort to reduce the clutter. I was also greeted with a new sister, Charlene, who was born on St. Patrick's Day of that year and was being hovered over by both parents. I was apprised of the epic trials they had endured in this performance as if it were in some way my responsibility. I was also warned of her frailty and cautioned that I would have to be quiet so as not to disturb her, or specifically them, when I entered the house at night. As if I needed the instruction! I determined not to allow this to interfere with future relations with Charlene and promised to follow their dictates as best I could. Then I was greeted by the statement that all the funds I had sent home were spent and that I had better find a job immediately. Gosh, it was great to be home again!

At any rate, I managed with what clothes I had purchased in Frisco, supplemented with a few local purchases, and sauntered down to the old haunts of Montpelier to greet friends and acquaintances. It was a strange time everywhere, as servicemen were returning daily in dribs and drabs. Familiar faces appeared at the old haunts. Many veterans taking advantage of the G. I. Bill began attending Vermont College. Norwich, too, was swamped, as were all colleges across the country. Back pay and bonuses arrived from Uncle Sam, and applications were made to the State of Vermont for their service bonus. All seemed to be flush for the moment. Everyone signed up for what became known as the 52-20 Club, a government program that gave $20 a week for up to a year for those not yet employed.

One of the articles of clothing I had purchased in San Francisco was a baby blue cardigan jacket with shoulder pads that extended a full one and a half inches beyond the point of my shoulders. The cardigan style was unusual, everyone being tuned to jackets with rather wide lapels, and this one had no lapels at all. When I wore this jacket, combined with the weight I was carrying at the time and being in fairly good shape due to exercise, I gave the impression of being a body builder. This elicited much comment, particularly among the females from Vermont College who happened to be following me down the street. On one occasion as I approached the bank to make a deposit, I heard a voice from a group behind me exclaiming, "My God! Look at those shoulders!" It was a great ego builder, although knowing my secret it was somewhat diminished by my thoughts of "wait 'til I take it off!" It was certainly an attention getter, as no one had seen such, except in California, I'm sure. When the gang I hung with received inquiries from some of those girls who had taken notice, I received a ragging in spades from them, Frank Facini, Jr. in particular.

Frank would swap jackets with me and, as he was much smaller, don mine, and strut around. The cardigan hung over him, the shoulder pads draped at about biceps level, and the jacket bottom hung like a skirt to almost his knees. He would hold his head high and demand that we address him as "Shoulders" as he pranced down the sidewalk. This brought much laughter from our crowd and quizzical glances from others, who undoubtedly wondered what we were up to. Frank even borrowed the "shoulders" jacket once when we double dated. That went over like a lead balloon! We sure had fun with that piece of clothing for many months until it became old hat and the gang's interest went on to new pursuits. I kept the jacket for many years until natural attrition destroyed its vitality and it went the way of all things.

Montpelier's environs at that time contained the greatest number of restaurants and bars, most of them run by Bill Sykas, one of my two godfathers. Bill owned the Victory Room, the Lobster Pot, the Miss Montpelier Diner, the East State Street Diner, and one other diner whose name escapes me. With the exception of Heney's diner and Brothers Café, this completed all the restaurants in the whole town. The Tavern Hotel and Pavilion were not included, as only transients would eat the poor fare they offered.

Bars frequented by the crowd of veterans were, aside from the VFW and American Legion, the Pavilion Grill, the Tavern Tap Room, Miller's Café (Lobster Pot), and the Victory Room. The Capital Spa and Ernie Handy's bar with their sawdust-dotted floors were considered the dives of that era, catering only to the dregs of society. Our preferences were the Pavilion Grill and the VFW, the Grill being our favorite haunt because the bartender was one of us. He attended Vermont College during the day. As most of the girls I had known were either off to college or had left the area for one reason or other, the only source for dating purposes were the girls at Vermont College. I, along with all the others, was drawn to the dormitories of Seminary Hill.

I had been home only a month or so and had not decided what I wanted to do in life and knew that I would receive no help from home if I went to college on the G.I. Bill. I heard that Joseph Foti, a Montpelier attorney, had bought Haskin's Pharmacy and that he was looking for someone to apprentice in pharmacy. I had become acquainted with Joe when he had chaperoned dances at one of the city clubs and thought I would apply, as I was getting tired of being on the 52-20 Club and needed something to do. I applied at the store where, because of my status as a vet, Joe hired me on the spot and I started the next day. Joe, I am sure, was influenced by my veteran status above all other considerations, as it meant that under the G.I. Bill the government would pay part of my salary. I had no idea that I would spend the next 40 plus years there.

Sam Foti, Joe's brother, had served in the Army, joining up in the years prior to the war and had reached the rank of First Lieutenant by remaining in the active reserve. Sam had been in the medical corps during his active service and, in addition to being manager of the store, was also apprenticed, as I was, to J. Wilsie Brisbin, a pharmacist pulled out of retirement by Joe.

At first I was assigned the menial tasks associated with the running of a drugstore, which included helping on the soda fountain at busy periods and making sandwiches for the noon trade. I also had the responsibility of dusting the merchandise, sweeping and mopping of floors, and window washing as the need arose. I also learned how to wait on customers and how to operate the two cash registers in the store. After about two weeks, the books I was required to study arrived, along with a course of study, and my apprenticeship began.

Mr. Haskins, the former owner of the store, had built his business in the sale of cosmetics and the fountain business. Consequently, his prescription business was at a definitely low point. If we filled one or two prescriptions a day, we were lucky, an exceptional day being one in which four or five were filled. Sam and Joe wanted to change this, but it was an uphill battle as the small hole in the wall store down the street, Everett's Pharmacy, had the bulk of the prescription business and was maintaining it. Several strategies were tried to pull that business to us but to little avail, until the death of Mr. Everett and the demise of his assistant John changed the established pattern.

Because of my work at the fountain, I renewed acquaintance with all the telephone people I had known in my youth, as the telephone office was situated in the floors above the store in the same block. Kate Colombo was still chief operator and she and others I knew had breaks during the day that they spent at our soda fountain. I got to know people who were regular customers and soon developed friendships with them in the course of conversation and general kidding that prevailed. Among them was the jeweler two doors up State Street, Philip Broe, a suave and sophisticated gentleman who always had an interesting story to tell. I liked Phil and spent several minutes of each day talking with him in the course of serving coffee, milkshakes, ice cream and the other goodies that constituted the fare we offered.

One day as I puttered washing glasses in the fountain sink, Phil rushed in the door, shouting that he had just been robbed. I dropped my towel and ran out the door as he pointed to a man running down State Street. Giving it no further thought, I raced after him, caught up as he crossed the bridge, hit him in the back with a tackle and rolled up to grasp his arms. At first, he tried to struggle but soon gave up, and as I raised him to his feet seemed to be trying to reach in his jacket pocket. I grabbed that hand in a judo lock and he became quite cowed. I turned and led him back up State Street to meet Phil, who now stood in front of his store.

As I arrived in front of the store, two policemen ran up and took charge of my prisoner. After a short conversation with them, I returned to my store and the waiting dishes. Phil came into the store after about a half hour's time and thanked me for stopping the thief. He told me the police had extracted a gun from the thief's jacket pocket before leading him away. It was only then that I realized that was what he had been reaching for when we were struggling. I thought no more of it until I was reminded of it long years afterward by the Braziers, who had found an old newspaper clipping telling of the affair. Phil and I became good friends, and I'm sure it helped when I went to him to purchase an engagement ring sometime later.

Only two incidents need to be told of the year 1948. The first was when I was talked into a free fall jump at the local airport at an air show in the spring which, although successful, completed my desire for jumping out of aircraft learned in Japan and I hung up my tools, so to speak. The other occurred while dating a girl from Vermont College. Arthur Comolli, his date, my date, and I were all riding in Hugh Jones' father's convertible Cadillac when Hugh (Bucko) and his date left Vermont College on our way to Barre for some function. We picked up my date last on West Street, headed over to Ridge Street, then down over Charles Street, one of the steepest streets in the city, top down and feeling swelled up at being transported in such class.

We negotiated the first part of the hill all right, but as we passed the entrance of Foster Street, Bucko swore and hollered we had no brakes. Down we roared to intersect Barre Street, our hearts in our throats, and thoughts of sure death swirled in our minds. Luckily, no cars appeared as we whipped straight across Barre Street into the entrance of one of the many stone sheds that lined the railroad tracks beyond. Nothing stood in our way as we shot down that short dirt road, then left the ground in a short jump caused by the embankment at the road's end. We landed between tracks, the front wheels touching first, then bounced across two more sets of tracks before coming to rest across a fourth set, where we sat stunned and unhurt. I don't know how we survived, as there were no seat belts in those days and all we could do was hang on to what part of the car we could, as well as each other. By some miracle, no one fell out and the only damage was to the car itself, which sat astride the tracks tilted on blown front tires. Buck's sister arranged for the car's removal and we walked, shaken, to the Pavilion Grill.

60

One evening in January, Don Lyons and I, having made prior arrangements to be picked up by Dick Campbell and others of our group, went skating at the rink on Vermont College campus. There I met a saucy girl I had seen around town but had not met before. We bumped into each other skating and, by way of introduction, I was slapped in the face and called egotistical which, instead of turning me off, intrigued me greatly and piqued my interest. When Dick showed up, I begged off and stayed behind to skate with this girl. Thus started my last romantic spree. We dated for some months. I met her parents after a basketball tournament where her father coached the winning team in their class, and in the spring became engaged.

On reflection, I would say that the qualities I saw in Lois were her forthrightness, honesty, and vivacious manner, along with a certain physical attraction that led me to fall in love. She also had a sense of humor, which I prized highly, for I knew she would need one of uncommon breadth if she went through the rest of life with me. It was not until much later that I learned that what I had thought forthrightness was stubbornness, and vivaciousness was child-like behavior, but by then I was trapped and still loved her anyway. So after a short courtship, we were married in Island Pond in August of that year.

Mother, in the meantime, had found a vague reason, never explained, for a new tiff with Grandmother and others of the Ewen clan and had ordered them to find new lodging. This left the upstairs apartment unused, and plans were made for Lois and I to rent the soon-to-be-vacated space. Returning home from our honeymoon, we entered our apartment, newly furnished, and proceeded into a new mode of life for the both of us—in debt for that furniture. Lois went back to her job as Secretary to the Dean of Education at Vermont College and I reluctantly went back to Foti Drug Store.

Lois' father Pop, in what I assume was frustration brought on by his having to come all the way from Island Pond to pick us up for weekend visits, found our first car for us. It was a 1940 Ford coupe, a two door vehicle much used but restored to usable shape by a friend of his, and once again we were in debt. Channing Haskell, a friend of mine, put me through the course of learning to drive it, and with further help from Joan Aguirre, I managed to get my license. That fall, I bagged my first deer and carried it proudly home tied across the fender of our car like some trophy of a medieval war, posing for a picture that depicts the arrogance of my youth.

Things at the store became more hectic and confused as the Korean War broke out and both Sam Foti and I received notice of call-up. I think Sam by that time had become disenchanted with both the hours of drug store life and the annoyance of dealing with the public and decided to take this opportunity to re-enter the service. This left only me to run the store under the auspices of J. Wilsie's license and so, when repeated orders arrived for me to report for duty, Joe Foti arranged deferments with the selective service board until my required time of reserve duty passed. It was an agonizing time for Lois and myself, as orders would arrive and we would plan on my leaving, only to be delayed by the deferments. Then a sense of calm, punctuated by anxiety, would prevail until the next missive. We had all been told that only by an Act of Congress and a declaration of war by that body would we reservists be called to service, and then only the single men. Since, with the birth of our son, we now were a family, we felt betrayed by the bureaucracy. At any rate, the time passed over a period of about a year and we went on with our lives as best we could. In the spring of 1952, I completed my requirements for license as a Registered Pharmacist.

61

Mother and Larry decided to sell the house on Ridge Street, so it was only a matter of time before we had to move. Knowing this, we started looking for ourselves, knowing also that we had two choices, one being to find an apartment somewhere else, the other being the better choice of finding a home of our own. The house we chose, mainly because we thought we could afford it, had at one time been the parsonage for the Methodist Church and had last been occupied by the Cranes. Charlie Crane was the author of a book very popular in those days, *Let Me Show You Vermont*, the contents of which can readily be discerned by its title. The house was large even by today's standards, having eight rooms with high ceilings situated around a massive hallway. It encompassed two floors, with an attic of such proportions as to have room for a full third floor if it were finished as such. The entire house was supported on a foundation of huge granite blocks forming a high-ceilinged basement, or cellar.

This imposing structure, placed on a high, banked lot that rose above the level of Hubbard Street and the plateau on which the Union Elementary School rested, was reached by a series of wooden steps set in the bank that reached from the sidewalk to the front porch. A precipitous driveway that started at street level and rose in a dogleg to the right reached the back. A garage, which at some time stored only a carriage and was too small to house a car, stood rather precariously on granite piers, slanted by the movement of the earth and frosts of previous winters, all the way to the bank that rose above it on its left side. It tilted so much it started leaning on the house and we had to remove it, after fulfilling all the city ordinances to get permission, as well as permission from the bank that held our loan.

We moved into this monster and rattled about its interior for part of a year, a family of only three in the beginning. The atmosphere was filled with the echoes of footsteps in its sparsely furnished space. The furniture from our apartment spread about its cavernous space inadequately since our former space had only four rooms, but we did somehow make a home. Lois being pregnant when we settled in, we soon had another member to fill a vacant room and disrupt our nights.

During this period, we made the acquaintance of our neighbors on both sides. The ones on the left as you faced our home were the Greenbergs, Dot and Nate, and the ones on the right the Whitneys. Nate Greenberg was an active man with a great personality who operated an automotive store situated a few doorways down from the pharmacy. He was a daily visitor to the soda fountain. He was also a busy man much involved in community functions and fraternal orders of the area. He possessed a ready smile and humor as well as a kindness of heart, and was loved by all who knew him. His wife, Dot, was also very nice, particularly with Lee, our next born, as she became almost a grandmother to her. Their children were much older than ours, but what we saw of them showed their parent's influence, as they were pleasant and polite whenever we talked to them.

The Whitneys, Cliff and Betty, on the other side, were a gregarious couple with whom we became fast friends through common interests. Television was just making its way to our area and Cliff had purchased a large set, 21 inches, before which we would sit enthralled on a Saturday night. We watched the few news programs, the new variety shows such as Milton Berle and Ed Sullivan, and, the epitome of weekend entertainment, the wrestling matches that featured such notables as Gorgeous George, Antonio Rocca and others of that ilk. We, like others, believed these shows to be true sport and cheered the good guys as we duly booed the bad, waiting in anticipation for the coming matches. The topic of conversation on Mondays was about the weekend matches, and all their moves were discussed. It was some time before it dawned on us that we had been conned and that wrestling was but a show. In the meantime, we spent many pleasant evenings with the Whitneys watching the tube and stuffing ourselves with goodies.

We were given our first family pet in the form of a female basset pup brought to us by the Brightenbacks who raised a litter. We named her MacDuff (Duff for short), all long floor-dragging ears, short legs and mournful face. Comical, with an appeal to every heart, she became the children's follower and footstool, lying in stoic silence as they stood on her body to reach higher for objects. Even in times when her actions annoyed us, such as following Lois' sister Gayle to church on Sundays and lying on the pulpit of Bethany Church, or when she escaped us and the police called me at the store to remove her from the intersection of Main and State Streets in Montpelier where she lay in its center with a bemused traffic cautiously driving around her, we forgave her with humor and love.

When I think back on the days spent in the house on Hubbard Street, I see Cam racing down those long stairs, across Hubbard Street and onto Park Avenue to the school grounds with enthusiasm for a day with his peers; a small, sweet child in a fake white fur coat complete with fur hat and mittens practicing her female wiles on all who viewed her; a young cowboy in blue jeans and flannel shirt, waist braced by a leather holster from which pistols show, complete with western hat; a waif with a red handkerchief filled with various and sundry treasures amongst which was a pack of cigarettes saved to appease her father in anticipation of being found by him when she ran away one day; a dining room window that cracked when being knocked on by Lois trying to warn baseball players on the lawn that they might break the window in the course of their game; and the long, sad time Lois spent with her dying mother as the tragedy of illness destroyed all feelings of home in the house and left us devastated and in search of another residence.

We moved into an old farmhouse just over the Montpelier town line into East Montpelier above the Kinstead and Towne Hills. I had explored this territory while looking for good fishing as a boy and knew its views of the Worcester range to the north, the Berlin hills to the west, and Trow Hill to the south. For the next twenty-five years I descended daily through the early morning mist from the hill into the valley to work in the pharmacy. Our lives changed completely as we acclimated to our new town, not far away distance-wise, but in another world altogether in the way we lived and brought up our children. We focused on renovating the house to accommodate our expanding family, on our children's schools and activities, and actively participated in the neighborhood and the town, as everything from road commissioner to member of the school board.

Eventually, the era of drugstore soda fountains made way for independent pharmacies and then chains. People had less and less time to stop by and sit in the old rocker with a cup of coffee we kept behind the counter for the regular characters from town and the doctors who would come by just to chat or do the crossword puzzle or get caught up on patients. Little by little, big drug company pills and prices and legislation replaced old-time remedies. One by one, those characters who had meant so much to me in my youth growing up in Montpelier found their way to Heaton House or a grown child's home or just faded away. As I look back at all I learned and all the people who influenced my life there, it wasn't such a bad place to grow up, after all.

0-595-33265-X

Printed in the United States
22394LVS00006B/326